YOUR recipe could appear in our next cookbook!

Share your tried & true family favorites with us instantly at
www.gooseberrypatch.com
If you'd rather jot 'em down by hand, just mail this form to...
Gooseberry Patch • Cookbooks – Call for Recipes
PO Box 812 • Columbus, OH 43216-0812

If your recipe is selected for a book, you'll receive a FREE copy!

Please share only your original recipes or those that you have made your own over the years.

Recipe Name:

Number of Servings:

Any fond memories about this recipe? Special touches you like to add
or handy shortcuts?

Ingredients (include specific measurements):

Instructions (continue on back if needed):

Special Code: **cookbookspage**

Over ➤

Extra space for recipe if needed:

Tell us about yourself...

Your complete contact information is needed so that we can send you your FREE cookbook, if your recipe is published. Phone numbers and email addresses are kept private and will only be used if we have questions about your recipe.

Name:
Address:
City: State: Zip:
Email:
Daytime Phone:

Thank you! Vickie & Jo Ann

Grandma's Favorites

Can't-miss recipes for delicious family dinners,
just like Grandma used to make.

Gooseberry Patch

An imprint of Globe Pequot
64 South Main Street
Essex, CT 06426

www.gooseberrypatch.com

1•800•854•6673

Copyright 2022, Gooseberry Patch 978-1-62093-486-9
Photo Edition is a major revision of **Grandma's Favorites**.

Do you have a tried & true recipe...

tip, craft or memory that you'd like to see featured in
a **Gooseberry Patch** cookbook? Visit our website at
www.gooseberrypatch.com and follow the
easy steps to submit your favorite family recipe.

Or send them to us at:

Gooseberry Patch
PO Box 812
Columbus, OH 43216-0812

Don't forget to include the number of servings your recipe makes,
plus your name, address, phone number and email address. If we
select your recipe, your name will appear right along with it...
and you'll receive a **FREE** copy of the book!

Contents

Dedication

For everyone who craves the old-fashioned comfort of sharing meals with family & friends...who know that the secret ingredient is love!

Appreciation

Our most heartfelt thanks to all of you who shared their family's cherished recipes, saved on index cards and scraps of paper.

Old-Fashioned
Breakfasts

Fluffy Baked Omelet

Nancy Wise
Little Rock, AR

I have fond memories of going out with my grandmother to gather eggs in the henhouse. Grandma knew lots of delicious ways to fix those eggs for breakfast...sometimes she'd add some snipped herbs from her garden or top them with a little cheese.

6 eggs, separated
1 T. all-purpose flour
1 T. cornstarch
1/2 t. salt

pepper to taste
1 c. milk
2 T. butter, melted

Whisk egg yolks in a large bowl. Add flour, cornstarch, salt and pepper; whisk until smooth. Whisk in milk gradually; set aside. In a separate deep bowl, beat egg whites with an electric mixer on high speed until stiff but not dry. Fold into egg yolk mixture. Spread melted butter in a 9" cast-iron skillet or round cake pan; pour in egg mixture. Bake, uncovered, at 350 degrees for 20 minutes, or until set. Turn omelet onto a warm platter; fold over. Makes 6 servings.

Make the most of scrambled farm-fresh eggs! If you like them fluffy, add a tablespoon of water for each egg. If creamy eggs are your favorite, whisk in some half-and-half. Cook over low heat in a dollop of butter, until set to desired firmness.

Grandma Flora's Potato Pancakes

Lisa Ann Panzino DiNunzio
Vineland, NJ

This is one of our family favorite recipes. So delicious warm or cold, topped with jam or apple butter...yum!

5 baking potatoes, peeled
   and grated
1/2 c. onion, grated
3 eggs, beaten
1/4 c. milk

1-1/2 c. all-purpose flour
1 t. salt
oil for frying
Optional: favorite jam, jelly or
   apple butter

In a large bowl, combine potatoes and onion; set aside. Whisk together eggs and milk in a separate bowl; add to potato mixture. Stir until blended. Add flour and salt; stir until a batter forms. To a large skillet, add about 1/4 inch oil; heat over medium-high heat. Carefully add several tablespoonfuls of batter per pancake to hot oil. Fry on each side until lightly golden. Remove to a paper towel-lined plate. Serve warm, plain or topped as desired. Makes 6 to 8 servings.

Keep shopping simple...create a shopping list that includes all the ingredients you normally use, plus a few blank lines for special items. You'll breeze right down the aisles!

Sleep-Over Breakfast Strata

Emily Martin
Ontario, Canada

Every year at Christmas, we're sure to have some of my relatives staying for the holidays. This recipe fills up our hungry crowd, and everyone loves it.

4 c. day-old white bread, cubed
8 eggs
1-1/2 c. milk
1/2 t. salt
1/2 t. pepper

8-oz. pkg. shredded Cheddar
   cheese
8-oz. pkg. sliced mushrooms
3/4 lb. bacon, crisply cooked
   and crumbled

Place bread in a 6-quart slow cooker sprayed with a non-stick vegetable spray; set aside. Beat eggs in a large bowl. Whisk in milk, salt and pepper; stir in cheese and mushrooms. Pour egg mixture evenly over bread; set aside. Cook bacon in a skillet over medium heat until crisp; drain, crumble and sprinkle over top. Cover and cook on low setting for 6 to 8 hours, until eggs have set and top is lightly golden. Uncover and let stand for several minutes before serving. Serves 8 to 10.

Vintage "day of the week" tea towels make the sweetest window valances...just drape them over the curtain rod. So cheerful!

Banana Crumb Muffins

Heidi Ladwig
Odebolt, IA

Whenever I make these muffins, no one believes me about how easy they are to make. Homemade is still the best! It's an awesome recipe to use up ripe bananas.

1-1/2 c. all-purpose flour
1 t. baking powder
1 t. baking soda
1/2 t. salt

3 ripe bananas, mashed
3/4 c. sugar
1 egg, lightly beaten
1/3 c. butter, softened

Combine flour, baking powder, baking soda and salt in a large bowl; whisk well. Add remaining ingredients; stir until well mixed and moistened. Spoon batter into greased or paper-lined muffin cups, filling 2/3 full. Sprinkle Crumb Topping evenly over muffins. Bake at 350 degrees for 18 to 20 minutes. Makes one dozen.

Crumb Topping:

1/3 c. brown sugar, packed
2 T. all-purpose flour

1/2 t. cinnamon
1 T. butter, softened

Combine all ingredients in a small bowl. Mix with a fork until crumbly.

Bananas will ripen quickly if placed in a
brown paper grocery bag overnight.

Grandmaw Lura's French Toast

Nancy Moffatt
Charleston, WV

This was my mother's favorite breakfast recipe. She always made it for us as kids.

6 eggs, beaten
2-1/2 c. half-and-half
1/2 c. honey
1-1/2 t. vanilla extract
2 t. orange zest

1/2 t. salt
8 to 10 slices Texas toast
   bread, cubed
1 c. raisins
Garnish: pecan syrup

In a large bowl, whisk together eggs and half-and-half. Stir in honey, vanilla, orange zest and salt; set aside. Spread bread cubes in a lightly greased 12"x9" baking pan; sprinkle with raisins. Pour egg mixture over top. Bake, uncovered, at 350 degrees for 45 minutes, or until puffed and golden. Serve with pecan syrup. Makes 8 servings.

Garden-fresh berries are luscious on waffles and pancakes. Just simmer fruit with a little sugar and a little water until it's syrupy. What a scrumptious way to start the day!

Jean's Scottish Oatcakes

Shirley Howie
Foxboro, MA

I have been making these for many years now for my hubby, who is of Scottish descent. They were a staple in his mom's kitchen, and now I am carrying on the tradition! They are really good with marmalade for breakfast. They also can do double duty as a savory snack or appetizer, topped with cheese or meat.

1 c. regular or quick-cooking oats, uncooked	1/4 t. salt
1 c. all-purpose flour	1/2 c. shortening
1/2 t. baking soda	2 to 3 T. cold water

In a bowl, combine oats, flour, baking soda and salt. Cut in shortening with a pastry blender or fork until mixture resembles fine crumbs. Add water, one tablespoon at a time, until a stiff dough forms. Turn dough out onto a lightly floured surface; roll to 1/8-inch thickness. Cut into 2-1/2 inch rounds with a biscuit or cookie cutter. Place on ungreased baking sheets. Bake at 375 degrees for 12 to 15 minutes, until starting to turn golden. Cool on a wire rack. Makes 1-1/2 dozen.

A great way to add toasty flavor to a favorite oatmeal recipe! Spread uncooked oats on a baking sheet and bake at 300 degrees for 8 to 10 minutes, until lightly golden. Let oats cool before combining with other ingredients.

Grandma's Coffee Cake

Julie Snow
Park Rapids, MN

I remember Grandma and Mom making this coffee cake when I was growing up. It was always a favorite and never lasted long!

3/4 c. shortening or lard
2 c. sugar, divided
3 c. all-purpose flour
1/8 t. salt
1 T. baking powder

4 eggs, beaten
12-oz. can evaporated milk
1 t. vanilla extract
1 T. Dutch baking cocoa
2 t. cinnamon

In a large bowl, blend shortening or lard and 1-1/2 cups sugar. Add flour, salt, baking powder, eggs, evaporated milk and vanilla. Beat well with an electric mixer on medium-high speed. Pour batter into a greased tube pan. For filling, mix remaining sugar, cocoa and cinnamon. Pour over batter; cut in filling with a knife. Bake at 350 degrees for one hour. Cool cake in pan on a wire rack. Serves 12.

Easy Crumb Cake

Mickey Jaimes
Monticello, IN

This is a recipe my grandmother used to make all the time. Our whole family loved it! Good for breakfast and for dessert too.

2 c. all-purpose flour
1-1/2 c. sugar
1/2 c. butter, melted
1/2 t. salt

cinnamon to taste
1 c. sour milk or buttermilk
1 t. baking soda
1 egg, beaten

In a large bowl, mix together flour, sugar, melted butter, salt and cinnamon until crumbly. Set aside 1/2 cup crumbs for topping. Add milk, baking soda and egg; stir until smooth. Pour batter into a greased 8"x8" baking pan; sprinkle with reserved crumbs. Bake at 350 degrees for 25 to 30 minutes. Makes 9 servings.

Cinnamon-Caramel Pull-Apart Bread

Leah Beyer
Columbus, IN

When I was growing up, my mom would make Monkey Bread. I remember loving it straight from the oven. I have created a similar recipe that I now make with my kids for weekend breakfasts.

1 c. sugar
2 t. cinnamon
1/2 c. butter
1/2 c. brown sugar, packed

1 T. water
1/4 t. salt
2 16.3-oz. tubes refrigerated
    jumbo biscuits, quartered

Combine sugar and cinnamon in a large plastic zipping bag; set aside. Melt butter in a small saucepan; add brown sugar, water and salt. Cook and stir over medium heat until mixture just begins to bubble and becomes a caramel sauce. Remove from heat. Pour 1/3 of sauce into a greased Bundt pan; set aside. Add half of quartered biscuits to sugar mixture in bag. Shake to cover completely; place biscuits on top of sauce in pan. Pour half of remaining sauce over biscuits. Repeat layering with remaining sugar mixture, biscuits and sauce. Bake at 350 degrees for 40 minutes. Let stand for 3 minutes; place a plate on top of pan and turn out biscuits with sauce onto plate. Serves 8.

A whistling teakettle adds cheer to any kitchen. It's easy to remove the hard water and lime build-up in a barn-sale find. Just pour in 2 cups of white vinegar and bring to a boil. Simmer for 10 minutes, then rinse well...all set to brew up a cup of tea!

Baked Eggs with 3 Cheeses

Debbie Keyes
Lafayette, IN

This is one of our family favorites for brunch gatherings.

7 eggs, beaten
1 c. milk
2 t. sugar
16-oz. pkg. shredded Monterey
    Jack or Muenster cheese
16-oz. container small-curd
    cottage cheese

1/2 c. cream cheese, cubed
2/3 c. butter, melted
1/2 c. all-purpose flour
1 t. baking powder

In a large bowl, whisk together eggs, milk and sugar. Add all cheeses and melted butter; mix well. Stir in flour and baking powder. Pour into a 3-quart casserole dish sprayed with non-stick vegetable spray. Bake at 350 degrees for 45 to 50 minutes, until a knife tip inserted in the center comes out clean. May be prepared ahead of time, covered and refrigerated. If put into oven directly from refrigerator, uncover and bake up to 60 minutes, until heated through. Makes 12 servings.

Save bacon drippings for adding flavor to other dishes. Just stir a couple tablespoons of reserved drippings into recipes such as cornbread, scrambled eggs, breakfast potatoes, greens or gravy.

Old-Fashioned
Breakfasts

Frozen Fruit Cups

Vicky Anderson
Perry, IA

I always made these for my niece and nephew for breakfast or a treat...they loved them! So refreshing and colorful, and you can take out just the number of cups you need at one time.

20-oz. can crushed pineapple
8-oz. pkg. frozen sliced
   strawberries, thawed
6-oz. can frozen lemonade
   concentrate, thawed
6-oz. can frozen orange juice
   concentrate, thawed

10-oz. jar maraschino cherries,
   drained and chopped
4 ripe bananas, chopped
2-1/2 c. cold water
1 c. sugar

Combine undrained pineapple and remaining ingredients in a large bowl; mix well. Spoon mixture into 30 paper-lined muffin cups. Cover and freeze. Let stand for 10 to 15 minutes before serving. Makes 2-1/2 dozen.

Wooden spoons make whimsical plant markers. Write the name on the bowl of each spoon with a permanent marker. A perfect use for old wooden spoons that can be scooped up for a song at tag sales!

Texas Potatoes

Lindsay Rupp
High Ridge, MO

My grandma always made this dish for us for Christmas morning breakfast. My cousins and I would load up our plates, leaving no room for anything else. It became a family tradition, served at birthday parties and other family get-togethers. It's not a holiday without Texas Potatoes!

2 c. corn flake cereal, crushed
1 c. butter, melted and divided
32-oz. pkg. frozen shredded
    hashbrowns, thawed
8-oz. pkg. shredded Cheddar
    cheese

16-oz. container sour cream
10-3/4 oz. can cream of
    mushroom soup
1 onion, chopped
1/8 t. pepper

Toss together cereal and 1/2 cup melted butter in a small bowl; set aside. In a large bowl, combine remaining butter and other ingredients. Mix well; transfer to a lightly greased 13"x9" baking pan. Spread reserved cereal mixture on top of casserole. Bake, uncovered, at 350 degrees for 45 minutes, or until hot and bubbly. Makes 10 servings.

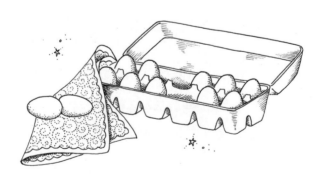

Grandma would love this new, no-fuss way to poach eggs. Add a tablespoon of water to a muffin cup and break in an egg. Repeat for as many as you want. Bake at 350 degrees for 11 to 13 minutes, until whites are set and yolks are as done as you like. Use a slotted spoon to serve eggs.

Old-Fashioned
Breakfasts

Best Breakfast Hash

Sarah Hente
Saint Charles, MO

This is really great for a hungry group! Serve with scrambled eggs for a complete hearty meal.

1 lb. ground pork breakfast
   sausage
4 potatoes, peeled and diced
1 onion, diced
1/4 c. butter, sliced

1 t. salt
1 t. pepper
1/2 t. onion powder
1/2 t. garlic powder
1/2 t. dried sage

Brown sausage in a large skillet over medium heat; drain. Add remaining ingredients. Cook, stirring occasionally, until potatoes are fork-tender and golden, 15 to 20 minutes. Makes 4 to 6 servings.

Homemade Breakfast Sausage

Dale Duncan
Waterloo, IA

My grandma used to make us this tasty sausage when we visited her on the farm. She always said, "Why buy it at the store when you can make it yourself?" Feel free to adjust the spices.

2 lbs. ground pork or turkey
1 T. brown sugar, packed
2 t. kosher salt
1-1/2 t. pepper

1-1/2 t. dried sage
1-1/2 t. dried thyme
1/2 t. dried marjoram
1/2 t. red pepper flakes

Combine all ingredients in a large bowl. Using your hands, mix well and shape into 8 flattened patties. For best flavor, wrap in plastic wrap; refrigerate overnight. Cook patties in a lightly greased large skillet over medium heat until golden and no longer pink in the center, 6 to 8 minutes. Makes 8 servings.

When breaking eggs, if a bit of shell gets into the bowl,
just dip a fingertip in water and pull it right out.

Peach Melba Pancakes

Sue Klapper
Muskego, WI

I love to treat my family & friends to a special brunch.

8-oz. can sliced peaches, drained
    and 2 T. syrup reserved
1 c. pancake & waffle mix
10 T. milk
1 egg, beaten
1 T. sugar

1 T. oil
10-oz. pkg. frozen sweetened
    raspberries, thawed
1 c. frozen whipped topping,
    thawed

Chop peach slices into small pieces; set aside. In a large bowl, combine pancake mix, milk, egg, sugar, oil and reserved peach syrup. Gently stir in chopped peaches. Spray a non-stick griddle with non-stick vegetable spray. Using 1/4 cup batter per pancake, cook on griddle until bubbly on the top and golden on the bottom. Turn and cook until other side is golden. Serve pancakes topped with raspberries and a dollop of whipped topping. Makes 7 to 8 pancakes; serves 4.

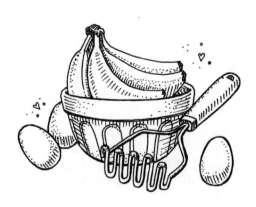

Did you know you can use ripe bananas for all or part of the liquid in pancake recipes? Just mash the bananas and stir in with the eggs. The end result is extra-moist pancakes loaded with flavor.

Old-Fashioned
Breakfasts

Cottage Cheese Pancakes

Julie Ann Perkins
Anderson, IN

Grandmothers are great! Both of mine clipped and saved recipes like this one that sparked their attention, then became family favorites.

1 c. plain yogurt
1 c. cottage cheese
1 T. sugar
1/4 t. salt

4 eggs, separated
1 to 1-1/2 c. all-purpose flour
Optional: powdered sugar

In a bowl, blend yogurt and cottage cheese. Add sugar, salt, egg yolks and enough flour to make a thin batter; mix well and set aside. In a separate bowl, beat egg whites with an electric mixer on high speed until stiff. Fold egg whites into yogurt mixture. Add batter by 1/4 cupfuls to a well-greased griddle over medium heat. Cook until golden on both sides. Top pancakes with Special Syrup. Dust with powdered sugar, if desired. Serves 2 to 4.

Special Syrup:

2 c. cranberry or blackberry juice   2 c. sugar

Combine juice and sugar in a saucepan. Bring to a boil over medium-high heat. Boil, stirring occasionally, until slightly thickened.

Making stacks of pancakes for a crowd? Keep them warm and yummy...just arrange pancakes on a baking sheet, set in a 200-degree oven, then serve as needed.

Grandma's Favorites

Sweet French Toast

Kathy Grashoff
Fort Wayne, IN

I used to make this for my boys when they were growing up. My mother-in-law gave me this recipe...I knew it was good because she made it for her own five children when they were growing up. So good!

1 c. milk
2 eggs
1/4 c. sugar
Optional: 1/2 to 1 t. cinnamon
    or nutmeg

10 to 12 slices white or
    wheat bread
Garnish: real maple syrup or
    powdered sugar

Whisk together milk, eggs, sugar and spice, if using. Spray a skillet with non-stick vegetable spray; heat over medium heat. Dip slices of bread in egg mixture; add to hot skillet. Cook until golden on the bottom; turn and cook again until golden. Serve topped with maple syrup or powdered sugar, as desired. Makes 4 to 6 servings.

Pannings' Pancakes

Cheryl Panning
Wabash, IN

As a young girl, I enjoyed being in the kitchen more than watching television. I found this recipe in an old schoolbook of my mother's and made this quite often for my dad. He loved them.

1 c. all-purpose flour
1 t. baking powder
2 T. sugar
1/2 t. salt

1 egg, well beaten
3/4 c. milk
3 T. shortening, melted

Combine flour, baking powder, sugar and salt; mix well. In a separate bowl, whisk together egg and milk; stir into flour mixture. Stir in shortening. Heat a lightly greased griddle or skillet over medium heat until drops of water sprinkled on griddle sizzle and disappear. Add batter, 1/4 cup per pancake. Cook until surface bubbles begin to break, one to 1-1/2 minutes. Turn; continue cooking until cooked through. Makes 4 servings.

Breakfasts

Puffy Oven Pancakes & Fruit

Annette Ingram
Grand Rapids, MI

Whenever we stayed overnight with my grandmother, she made us these sweet little individual pancakes for us. She called them "Dutch babies." Sometimes she added a dollop of whipped cream...such a treat!

2 eggs, lightly beaten
6 T. all-purpose flour
6 T. milk
1/4 t. salt

1/4 c. orange marmalade
1-1/3 c. sliced strawberries,
    kiwi fruit, nectarines and/or
    peaches

Lightly coat four, 10-ounce custard cups with non-stick vegetable spray; set aside. In a small bowl, whisk together eggs, flour, milk and salt until smooth. Immediately pour batter into custard cups; set on a baking sheet. Bake at 400 degrees for 15 to 20 minutes, until pancakes are puffed and golden. Meanwhile, place marmalade in a microwave-safe cup. Microwave, uncovered, for about 30 seconds, until melted. To serve, top puffed pancakes with fruit; spoon melted marmalade over fruit. Serve warm. Makes 4 servings.

Add a dash of whimsy to the breakfast table! Serve up pancake syrup or cream for cereal in Grandma's vintage cow-shaped creamer.

Bacon & Sausage Gravy

Mel Chencharick
Julian, PA

Most people I know serve this gravy over biscuits. Yes, that way is good, but I've found this gravy is also delicious over waffles, and is great over country-fried steak and mashed potatoes too. Serve it for breakfast, lunch and supper.

1 lb. ground pork sausage
5 slices thick-cut bacon, chopped
1/2 c. onion, chopped
2 cloves garlic, minced
3 T. all-purpose flour

16-oz. container half-and-half
1 t. salt
1 t. pepper
2 T. butter, sliced

In a large skillet over medium heat, combine sausage, bacon, onion and garlic. Cook for 8 to 10 minutes, until sausage is browned and crumbly. Stir in flour and cook for 2 to 3 minutes, stirring often. Gradually stir in half-and-half and seasonings. Cook for 3 to 4 minutes, until gravy is thickened. Remove from heat; stir in butter until melted. Makes 6 to 8 servings.

A cast-iron skillet is perfect for cooking up delicious breakfast foods. If your skillet hasn't been used in awhile, season it first...rub it all over with oil and bake at 300 degrees for an hour. Cool completely before removing from the oven.

Creamed Chipped Beef on Toast

Judy Schroff
Churubusco, IN

My mother used to make this quick & easy dish for breakfast...even for supper when time was short. A tasty stick-to-your-ribs meal anytime!

1/4 c. butter
3-oz. jar dried beef, cut into
   small pieces
1/4 c. all-purpose flour

2 c. milk
salt and pepper to taste
4 slices bread, toasted

Melt butter in a skillet over medium heat. Add beef; cook for several minutes. Blend in flour until smooth; slowly add milk. Cook over low heat until thickened, stirring constantly. Stir in seasonings. To serve, spoon mixture over slices of toast. Makes 4 servings.

Hang up an old-fashioned mini washboard where family messages, calendars and to-do lists can be easily found. Button magnets and clothespin clips can hold everything in place and add a dash of fun.

Butter Dip Biscuits

Dana Rowan
Spokane, WA

These biscuits are so easy to make, they are our go-to breakfast for Sunday morning! While the biscuits are baking, I whip up some homemade sausage gravy or set out the butter and jam. There are never any biscuits left...they are that good!

1/2 c. butter	4 t. sugar
2-1/2 c. all-purpose flour	1-3/4 c. buttermilk
4 t. baking powder	

Place butter in an 8"x8" baking pan. Heat in oven set at 350 degrees until melted. Meanwhile, combine flour, baking powder and sugar in a large bowl; mix well. Slowly stir in buttermilk. Dough will be slightly sticky. Press dough into pan over melted butter, using your hands. Some of the butter will come up over the top of the dough. Score dough into 9 square biscuits. Bake at 450 degrees for 20 to 25 minutes, rotating pan in oven after 10 minutes. Makes 9 biscuits.

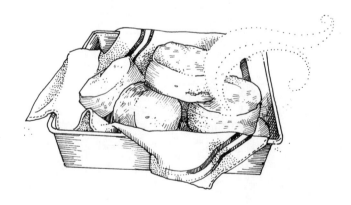

Grandma's secret for the flakiest biscuits? Just stir to moisten and gently roll or pat the dough...don't overmix it.

Old-Fashioned
Breakfasts

Aunt Millie's Strawberry Freezer Jam

Susan Munger
Ruskin, FL

My Aunt Millie used this same recipe for many many years. She said it brought back fond memories of when she was young. It's easy to make and very yummy.

2 c. strawberries, hulled
   and sliced
4 c. sugar
2 T. lemon juice

3-oz. pouch liquid fruit pectin
2 one-pint freezer containers
   with lids, sterilized

Place strawberries in a large bowl; mash well with a potato masher. Add sugar; mix very well. Let stand for 10 minutes. Add lemon juice; mix well. Add pectin; stir for 3 minutes. Ladle into freezer containers, leaving 1/2-inch headspace. Wipe rims; add lids. Let stand at room temperature for 24 hours. Cool, then freeze. Thaw in refrigerator to use. Makes 2 pints.

Aunt B's Peach Freezer Jam

Bryna Dunlap
Muskogee, OK

Like a spoonful of sunshine at breakfast!

12 ripe peaches, pitted, peeled
   and chopped
4 c. water
4-1/2 c. sugar

2-oz. pkg. dry pectin
4 one-pint freezer containers
   with lids, sterilized

In a large saucepan, combine peaches with enough water to just cover. Boil for 20 minutes over medium-high heat, or until peaches are softened. Stir in sugar; cook and stir until dissolved. Stir in pectin. Remove from heat after one minute. Ladle into freezer containers, leaving 1/2-inch headspace. Wipe rims; add lids. Let stand at room temperature for 24 hours. Cool, then freeze. Thaw in refrigerator to use. Makes 4 pints.

Stir a spoonful of homemade jam into warm breakfast oatmeal...yum!

Grandma's Favorites

Pecan-Raisin Cinnamon Rolls

Margaret Gravitt
Rising Fawn, GA

I have made these cinnamon rolls for more than 25 years. We all love them! We have four children, nine grandchildren and eighteen great-grandchildren, so I often double this recipe.

4 c. all-purpose flour, divided
1 c. sugar, divided
1-1/2 oz. env. active dry yeast
1-1/2 t. salt
1-2/3 c. water
1/2 c. oil

2 eggs, beaten
1/4 c. butter, melted
1-1/2 t. cinnamon
1/2 c. raisins
1/2 c. chopped pecans
Garnish: favorite vanilla icing

In a large bowl, combine one cup flour, 1/2 cup sugar, yeast and salt; set aside. In a saucepan over medium-low heat, heat water and oil to 120 to 130 degrees; remove from heat. Add hot water mixture to flour mixture; beat just until moistened. Add eggs; beat until smooth. Stir in enough of remaining flour to form a soft, sticky dough. Turn onto floured surface; knead until smooth, about 6 to 8 minutes. Cover with a tea towel; let stand for 15 minutes. Turn dough onto a floured surface; divide in half. Roll out each half into a rectangle, 24 inches by 15 inches. Brush with melted butter to within 1/2 inch of edges. Combine remaining sugar and cinnamon; sprinkle over dough. Sprinkle with raisins and pecans. Roll up each rectangle jelly-roll style, starting on one long edge; pinch ends to seal. Cut each roll into 12 slices. Place rolls in a greased 15"x10" jelly-roll pan. Cover and let rise in a warm place until double, about 30 minutes. Bake at 425 degrees for 18 minutes, or until golden. Cool; drizzle with Powdered Sugar Icing. Makes 2 dozen.

Powdered Sugar Icing:

2 c. powdered sugar
1/4 c. butter, softened

1 to 2 T. milk

Stir together all ingredients to a drizzling consistency.

Old-Fashioned *Breakfasts*

Old-Fashioned Hot Cocoa

Jennie Gist
Gooseberry Patch

I remember Mom making this hot cocoa for us five kids on winter days, back in the 1960s.

1/2 c. sugar
1/4 c. baking cocoa
1/8 t. salt
1/3 c. hot water

4 c. milk
3/4 t. vanilla extract
Garnish: marshmallows

In a large saucepan, stir together sugar, cocoa and salt; stir in water. Cook over medium heat, stirring constantly, until mixture comes to a boil. Cook and stir 2 minutes while boiling. Stir in milk; reduce heat to medium-low. Cook and stir until heated through, but do not boil. Remove from heat; add vanilla. Beat with a whisk until foamy. Serve topped with marshmallows. Makes 4 to 5 servings.

A buttery slice of old-fashioned cinnamon toast warms you right up on a chilly morning. Spread softened butter generously on one side of toasted white bread and sprinkle with cinnamon-sugar. Broil for one to 2 minutes, until hot and bubbly.

Great-Grandpa's Roll-Ups

Amy Gordon
Breezy Point, MN

My Great-Grandpa Ray used to make these every time my brothers and I came to visit! They are quick and delicious. After he passed on, my mom made them often at home. Now as a mom of five, I double the recipe and serve them with fresh fruit and whipped topping. Also try eggs and syrup! The options are endless and so are the memories.

1-1/2 c. all-purpose flour
2-1/4 c. milk
1 t. salt
3 eggs, beaten

1/3 c. oil
Garnish: softened butter,
    cinnamon-sugar, jam or jelly

In a bowl, mix together flour, milk and salt; stir in eggs and oil. Batter will be thin. Spray a large skillet with non-stick butter spray; heat over medium heat. Add batter by 1/3 cupfuls. Cook for about one minute on one side; turn over. Cook for 30 seconds on other side, or until golden. Spread with butter; sprinkle with cinnamon-sugar and roll up. Serve warm with desired toppings. Serves 6 to 8.

Baba's Milk Soup

Staci Prickett
Montezuma, GA

I have fond memories of this soup. When I was little, my Baba often made this Polish recipe for me for breakfast or as a snack. Baba always made it with noodles, but rice or oats are sometimes used.

4 c. milk
2 t. sugar
1 t. salt

2 to 3 c. kluski or medium egg
    noodles, uncooked
Garnish: 4 to 8 T. butter

In a large saucepan over medium heat, mix together milk, sugar and salt. Bring to a simmer but do not boil. Stir in noodles; simmer until tender. Ladle soup into bowls; top each bowl with one to 2 tablespoons butter. Makes 4 servings.

Old-Fashioned
Breakfasts

Shirley's Breakfast Casserole

Shirley Condy
Plainview, NY

*I make this recipe whenever I have guests, and it's always a hit.
Instead of bacon, you can use chopped breakfast sausage or baked
ham. Serve with warm buttered toast.*

6 slices bread, torn into chunks
8-oz. pkg. shredded Cheddar
   cheese
1 lb. bacon, crisply cooked
   and crumbled

6 eggs, beaten
2 c. milk

Place bread chunks in a 13"x9" baking pan. Sprinkle cheese and
bacon on top. Whisk together eggs and milk; pour over all. Cover
and refrigerate overnight. Bake, uncovered, at 350 degrees for about
one hour, until bubbly and golden. Makes 6 servings.

Candied Grapefruit

Jill Ball
Highland, UT

*This was my favorite childhood breakfast...we had this broiled
grapefruit at least once a week. Yummy and quick!*

2 grapefruit, halved
1 T. sugar

1 T. cinnamon, or to taste
4 t. butter, diced

Use a small serrated knife to cut the sections in the grapefruit halves.
Sprinkle each grapefruit half with desired amount of sugar and
cinnamon; dot with butter. Arrange grapefruit halves on a broiler pan.
Broil under preheated broiler for 3 to 5 minutes, until butter melts and
sugar starts to turn golden. Serves 4.

Keep a cherished cookbook spatter-free!
Slip it into a gallon-size plastic zipping
bag before cooking up a favorite recipe.

Date & Nut Bran Muffins

Anne Girucky
Cape Coral, FL

I have been making these muffins for quite some time. They're great with cinnamon cream cheese and a cup of hot coffee.

1/2 c. butter
1-1/2 c. chopped dates
1/2 t. vanilla extract
1 egg, beaten
1 c. cake flour
1 c. oat bran
4 t. baking powder

1/4 t. salt
Optional: 1/4 c. brown sugar,
    packed
1 c. milk, divided
3/4 c. chopped pecans
1/4 c. rolled oats, uncooked

In a large bowl, beat butter with dates until butter is light; beat in vanilla. Add egg and blend well. In another bowl, combine flour, bran, baking powder, salt and brown sugar, if using; mix until blended. Add milk; fold in with a spatula just until a lumpy batter comes together. Fold in pecans. Spoon batter into paper-lined muffin cups, filling 2/3 full. Sprinkle muffins with oats. Bake at 400 degrees for 30 minutes, or until golden. Let cool 5 minutes before removing from pan. Makes one dozen.

Fresh-baked muffins, anytime! Place cooled muffins in a freezer bag and freeze. To serve, wrap individual muffins in aluminum foil and pop into a 300-degree oven for a few minutes, until toasty warm.

Old-Fashioned
Breakfasts

Dad's Blueberry Muffins

Susan Vinson
Columbia, SC

Every Christmas, my mother baked these muffins for breakfast. The aroma of the muffins baking always added to the excitement of Christmas morning. But they're too good to eat just once a year! They bring back memories of the wonderful cook she was.

2 c. biscuit baking mix
1/4 c. plus 2 T. sugar, divided
1/2 t. cinnamon
8-oz. container sour cream

1 egg, beaten
1 c. fresh or frozen blueberries,
    thawed if frozen and drained

In a large bowl, combine biscuit mix, 1/4 cup sugar and cinnamon; mix well. Make a well in the center; add sour cream and egg. Beat with a fork until well combined. Gently fold blueberries into batter. Lightly grease 12 muffin cups. Scoop 1/4 cup batter into each muffin cup. Sprinkle muffins with remaining sugar, 1/2 teaspoon per muffin. Bake at 425 degrees for 20 minutes, or until golden. Makes one dozen.

A baker's secret! Grease muffin cups on the bottoms and just halfway up the sides. The muffins will bake up nicely puffed on top.

Anything Goes Quiche

Cathy Hillier
Salt Lake City, UT

Gram was always thrifty, using bits of this & that to create the most delicious dishes for us. Holiday ham often went into her quiche, but she also used leftover party shrimp or a few slices of crisp bacon from yesterday's breakfast. In springtime, a few spears of chopped asparagus were a must too. Never the same, but always tasty!

9-inch pie crust, unbaked
3 eggs, beaten
1-1/2 c. milk
1 T. all-purpose flour
1/4 t. salt
1/8 t. nutmeg

1/2 c. cooked ham, diced
1-1/2 c. shredded Swiss cheese
1/2 c. shredded Monterey Jack cheese
Optional: fresh parsley, cherry tomatoes

Bake pie crust according to package directions; set aside. Meanwhile, in a large bowl, combine eggs, milk, flour and seasonings. Add ham and cheeses; mix well. Spoon mixture into warm pie crust. Cover the edge of crust with a strip of aluminum foil. Bake at 325 degrees for 35 to 40 minutes. Remove foil; bake another 10 to 15 minutes, until a knife tip inserted in the center tests clean. Let stand 5 to 10 minutes before slicing. Garnish with parsley and cherry tomatoes, if desired. Makes 6 servings.

Keep tea towels handy on a peg rack...stitch a folded loop of rick rack to one corner of the towels for hanging.

Chill-Chasing
Soups & Breads

Nonnie's Italian Chicken Soup

Jaki Browne
Conway, NH

I have fond memories of being a young child and visiting my Nonnie's (grandmother's) house, the aroma of her homemade soup wafting through her house and the wonderful flavor of the soup as I sat at her kitchen table. Years later, as a teen, I remember the same aromas and taste of homemade soup from my Italian mom's kitchen, especially if there was a threat of a cold coming on. As an adult, I followed the tradition with my own children. Even now, my children and grandchildren often request my own homemade Nonnie Soup.

4 to 5-lb. chicken, cut up
28-oz. can crushed tomatoes
   with Italian herbs
2 stalks celery, diced
2 onions, diced
4 carrots, peeled and sliced

1-1/2 t. Italian seasoning
1/2 t. garlic powder
1/4 t. dried thyme
1 c. pastina pasta, uncooked
Garnish: grated Parmesan cheese

Place chicken in a Dutch oven; add enough water to cover chicken. Add tomatoes with juice, vegetables and seasonings. Bring to a boil over high heat; reduce heat to medium-low. Simmer until chicken is very tender, stirring occasionally, about 1-1/2 hours. Remove chicken to a platter, reserving broth. Allow chicken to cool; remove chicken from bones and return to broth in Dutch oven. In a separate saucepan, cook pastina according to package directions. Add cooked pastina to soup. Serve with Parmesan cheese. Makes 10 to 12 servings.

Chicken backs and wings are excellent for making rich, flavorful broth. Save up unused ones in the freezer until you have enough for a pot of broth.

Chill-Chasing
Soups & Breads

Filé Chicken & Sausage Gumbo

Betty Kozlowski
Newnan, GA

*This is the meal we came home to from church every Sunday.
Though there are many variations, my grandmother's and
mom's gumbo was simple, yet unbelievably good.*

1/4 c. oil
3 T. all-purpose flour
10 c. water
1-1/2 lbs. chicken pieces
1 lb. smoked pork sausage, sliced

1/4 c. onion, chopped
1/4 c. shallots, chopped
1/4 c. fresh parsley, chopped
salt to taste
cooked rice

Combine oil and flour in a large soup pot over low heat. Cook over low heat, stirring constantly, until mixture is dark brown. Be careful not to allow it to burn. Slowly stir in water until mixture is smooth. Add remaining ingredients except rice. Bring to a boil over high heat; reduce heat to medium-low. Cover and simmer for one to 2 hours, stirring often. If desired, debone chicken and return meat to the pot. Serve over cooked rice. Makes 6 servings.

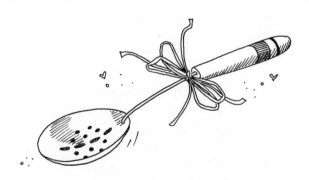

Here's a simple trick to skim the fat from a pot of soup. Place a metal spoon in the freezer. When the soup is done, use the chilled spoon to skim the surface...the fat will stick to the spoon.

Grandmother's Chicken Noodle Soup

Mary King
Ashville, AL

Grandmother used to make this soup whenever anyone was sick. She said it was made with chicken and noodles and lots of love...that was the secret ingredient. She also said that this is the easiest soup to make right out of the pantry. Now it is time to get a bowl and help yourself to a great soup.

2 to 3 boneless, skinless chicken
  breasts
4 c. water
15-oz. can sweet peas, drained
2 14-1/2 oz. cans sliced carrots,
  drained
1/4 c. butter

1 t. garlic powder
salt and pepper to taste
12-oz. pkg. medium egg noodles,
  uncooked
Optional: 1 to 2 14-oz. cans
  chicken broth

In a soup pot, combine chicken and water. Bring to a boil over medium-high heat. Cook for 35 to 45 minutes, until chicken is cooked through. Remove chicken to a plate to cool, reserving broth in soup pot. Add peas, carrots, butter and seasonings to reserved broth. Cut chicken into bite-size pieces and add to broth. Bring back to a boil and add desired amount of noodles; cook until noodles are soft. If more broth is desired, add optional broth, one can at a time, to desired consistency; warm through. Makes 6 to 8 servings.

Warm-from-the-oven rolls deserve a crock of herb butter! Blend one cup butter with 2 tablespoons fresh parsley, one tablespoon minced garlic and 2 teaspoons fresh oregano.

Chill-Chasing
Soups & Breads

Grandma's Sunday Rolls

Cherrie Fulton
Merrimack, NH

*We would all gather at Grandmother's house for Sunday dinner.
Before church, she would make these rolls with a little help from the
grandchildren. I have continued making them for our Sunday dinners
and other special times when we all get together. The smell of these
rolls baking brings my family running!*

1 env. active dry yeast	1 t. salt
1/4 c. plus 1/8 t. sugar, divided	1/4 c. oil
1/4 c. warm water, 110 to 115	1 egg, beaten
degrees	3-1/2 c. all-purpose flour,
1 c. milk	divided

Add yeast and 1/8 teaspoon sugar to warm water; let stand for several
minutes. Meanwhile, microwave milk in a microwave-safe cup for
2 minutes. Pour milk into a large bowl and add salt; stir in remaining
sugar, oil and egg. Mix well and let cool to lukewarm. Stir one cup flour
into milk mixture; add yeast mixture and stir well. Gradually add
remaining flour. Cover and let stand for 2 hours in a warm place. Punch
down dough. On a floured surface, roll out dough 3/4-inch thick; cut
into 3 to 4-inch circles with a biscuit cutter. Fold each dough circle in
half; place on a parchment paper-lined baking sheet. Cover and let rise
for 2 hours. Bake at 350 degrees for 12 minutes, or until golden. Makes
1-1/2 dozen.

Take a little time to share family traditions with your kids and grandkids!
A cherished family recipe can be a great conversation starter at dinner.

Farmer Sausage & Green Bean Soup

Wendy Manz
Manitoba, Canada

Some of the fondest memories of my childhood come from the evening meals and the beautiful aroma of spices in my mother Irene's kitchen. Mom made this hearty soup for our evening meal many times when I was growing up. I make it now with some variations, and my husband really enjoys it too. Help yourself to second and third bowls!

10 c. water
5 6-inch sections farmer sausage
   or other smoked pork
   sausage
9 potatoes, peeled and cubed
3-1/2 c. fresh green beans,
   trimmed and cut, or 2 15-oz.
   cans cut green beans, drained

Optional: 1 c. carrots, peeled
   and diced
1/2 c. fresh Italian parsley,
   chopped
1/2 t. dried sage
1/2 t. dried basil
1 whole star anise
5 bay leaves

In a large soup pot over high heat, bring water to a boil. Add all ingredients except star anise and bay leaves; reduce to medium heat. Place star anise and bay leaves in a spice ball or tea strainer; add to soup pot. Simmer for one hour or a little longer, stirring occasionally. Taste and adjust seasonings; if soup is becoming too spicy, remove spice ball or add a little more water. Makes 8 servings.

A well-loved china teapot that's been handed down to you makes a sweet vase for garden roses, daffodils or daisies.

Pork & Mushroom Stew

*Judy Henfey
Cibolo, TX*

I first tasted this stew as a teenager. My aunt's friend Linda lived in an old farmhouse, where she grew all of her own vegetables and herbs and made lots of crafts. She had no children and always had my aunt and me come over to her home. We'd spend hours in the kitchen trying new recipes. We had so much fun...I thought she was the hippest woman around!

3 to 4-lb. pork butt, cubed
2 T. canola oil
2 c. onions, chopped
4 8-oz. cans tomato sauce
2 6-oz. cans tomato paste
5-1/2 c. water

3 green peppers, chopped
1 c. celery, chopped
1/2 lb. sliced mushrooms
garlic powder to taste
dried basil to taste
salt and pepper to taste

In a large soup pot over medium-high heat, brown pork cubes in oil. Remove pork to a large plate. Add onions to drippings in skillet; sauté until translucent. Return pork to soup pot. Add tomato sauce, tomato paste and water; stir well. Simmer over medium-low heat, stirring occasionally, for 45 minutes. Add remaining ingredients. Continue simmering until vegetables are tender, about 1-1/2 to 2 hours. Makes 8 servings.

Grandma's stove always had a pot of savory soup bubbling on a back burner. Cook up the same slow-simmered flavor with your slow cooker! A favorite soup recipe that simmers for one to 2 hours on the stove can cook for 6 to 8 hours on the low setting without overcooking.

Zucchini Garden Chowder

Barb Bargdill
Gooseberry Patch

My family discovered this recipe some years ago and we've been making it ever since. In the summertime, ripe tomatoes and sweet corn from the garden go into the pot along with the zucchini.

1/3 c. butter
2 zucchini, chopped
1 onion, chopped
4 T. fresh parsley, minced and divided
1 t. Italian seasoning
1/3 c. all-purpose flour
1 t. salt
1/4 t. pepper
3 c. water

3 cubes chicken or vegetable bouillon
1 t. lemon juice
14-1/2 oz. can diced tomatoes
10-oz. pkg. frozen corn
12-oz. can evaporated milk
1 c. shredded Cheddar cheese
1/4 c. grated Parmesan cheese
1/8 t. sugar

Melt butter in a Dutch oven over medium heat. Add zucchini, onion, 2 tablespoons parsley and Italian seasoning; sauté for several minutes, until tender. Stir in flour, salt and pepper. Gradually stir in water. Add bouillon and lemon juice; mix well. Bring to a boil; cook and stir for 2 minutes. Add tomatoes with juice, corn and evaporated milk; return to a boil. Reduce heat; cover and simmer for 5 minutes, or until corn is tender. Just before serving, stir in cheeses and sugar. Garnish bowls with remaining parsley. Makes 8 to 10 servings.

Save those leftover fresh herbs for later use. Spoon chopped herbs into an ice cube tray, one tablespoon per cube. Cover with water and freeze. Frozen cubes can be dropped right into dishes as they cook.

Chill-Chasing
Soups & Breads

Garden-Fresh Tomato Soup

JoAnn
Gooseberry Patch

A grilled cheese sandwich's best friend.

4 c. ripe tomatoes, chopped
1 slice onion, coarsely chopped
2 c. chicken broth
4 whole cloves

2 T. butter
2 T. all-purpose flour
1 t. salt
2 t. sugar

In a soup pot over medium heat, combine tomatoes, onion, broth and cloves. Bring to a boil; reduce heat to medium-low and simmer for 20 minutes. Discard cloves. In a blender, process soup in batches to desired consistency; set aside in a bowl. In the same soup pot, melt butter over medium heat. Stir in flour; cook and stir for several minutes, until mixture is a medium brown. Gradually whisk in a bit of the the soup until smooth; stir in remaining soup and heat through. Season with salt and sugar. Makes 6 servings.

Mimi Charlotte's Walnut Loaf

Patty Flak
Erie, PA

This is an old recipe my grandmother used to make. It's super easy and really tasty any time of day.

2 c. all-purpose flour
3/4 c. sugar
4 t. baking powder
1 t. salt

1/4 c. shortening
1 egg, beaten
1 c. milk
1 c. chopped walnuts

Mix flour, sugar, baking powder and salt in a large bowl. Cut in shortening with a fork. Add egg and milk; stir just until moistened. Fold in walnuts. Pour batter into a greased 9"x5" loaf pan. Bake at 400 degrees for 40 to 45 minutes. Immediately remove from pan; cool on a wire rack. Makes one loaf.

Ham & Bean Soup

Bethi Hendrickson
Danville, PA

This Pennsylvania Dutch soup was always a staple in our home. It is the perfect comfort food on cold winter evenings. This recipe keeps well in the refrigerator for a few days, or freeze the leftovers for a later meal. Serve hot with a slice of crusty bread.

1-1/2 to 2 lbs. ham hocks or
    cooked ham steak, cubed
2 40-oz. cans Great Northern
    beans
1/2 lb. baby carrots, sliced

4 stalks celery, chopped
3 to 4 potatoes, peeled and cubed
2 T. ham soup base
Optional: 12-oz. can regular or
    non-alcoholic beer

Add ham hocks or cubed ham to a large stockpot; add enough water to half-fill the pot. Bring to a boil over medium-high heat. Reduce heat to medium-low and simmer for 30 minutes, or until ham is very tender. If using ham hocks, remove from pot; shred meat with a fork and return to liquid in pot. Add undrained beans, carrots, celery, potatoes and soup base; stir well. Reduce heat to low; simmer for one hour, stirring occasionally. Add beer, if using; simmer for an additional one to 2 hours. Makes 15 to 20 servings.

Watch for old-fashioned clear glass canisters at tag sales and flea markets...perfect countertop storage for all kinds of pasta.

Chill-Chasing
Soups & Breads

Sweet Cornbread

Arlene Coury
San Antonio, TX

You may ask yourself, Is this cornbread or cake? Its sweet, delicate flavor is that good! It is even more special to me because I bake it in a cast-iron skillet that belonged to my grandmother, to whom I was very close. I have many fond memories of her.

1/4 c. butter, sliced	1 T. baking powder
1 c. cornmeal	1 egg, beaten
1 c. all-purpose flour	1 c. milk
1 c. sugar	1 t. vanilla extract

Melt butter in a cast-iron skillet at 350 degrees in oven. Meanwhile, in a large bowl, mix cornmeal, flour, sugar and baking powder. Stir egg into flour mixture. Add milk and vanilla; stir until well combined. Pour batter into hot skillet. Bake at 350 degrees for 20 to 25 minutes, until a toothpick inserted in center comes out clean. Makes 8 servings.

Grandmother could always be found wearing her apron...why not revive this useful tradition? Look through flea markets for some of the prettiest vintage aprons, or find a fun pattern and stitch one up in an afternoon.

Dad's White Chili

Jennifer Yaney
Floyds Knob, IN

We often request this chili when my father-in-law is cooking for us.
It's a unique change from the usual tomato-based chili.

2 c. onions, finely chopped
4 cloves garlic, minced
1 T. oil
2 15-1/2 oz. cans cannellini or
   white kidney beans
2 15-1/2 oz. cans white shoepeg
   corn, drained
3 c. cooked chicken, chopped
32-oz. can low-sodium chicken
   broth

15-oz. jar white Monterey Jack
   queso dip
7-oz. can chopped green chiles
2 t. ground cumin
1 t. dried parsley
1 t. dried oregano
Optional: 1 t. caramel popcorn
   seasoning

In a large stockpot over medium heat, sauté onions and garlic in oil until tender. Stir in undrained beans and remaining ingredients. Simmer over medium-low heat until heated through, about 20 minutes. Makes 8 servings.

Seasoned Cornbread

Irene Robinson
Cincinnati, OH

A nice change from plain cornbread, and so simple.

8-1/2 oz. pkg. corn muffin mix
1/2 t. poultry seasoning

1 egg, beaten
2/3 c. milk

Combine muffin mix and seasoning in a bowl. Add egg and milk; stir just until moistened. Pour batter into a well-greased 8"x8" baking pan. Bake at 400 degrees for 18 to 20 minutes, until golden. Serve warm. Makes 9 servings.

Get rid of that smell on your hands after chopping onions. Simply hold your hands under cold running water while rubbing them with a stainless steel spoon.

Soups & Breads

Darn Good Chili

Alyssa Payne
Magnolia, TX

This is one of my grandma's recipes. We have enjoyed it as a family for many years, whether we were out camping or at home on a chilly day.

1 lb. ground beef
1/2 onion, diced
1/2 green pepper, diced
8-oz. can tomato sauce
2 c. water
1 T. chili powder

1 t. ground cumin
1/2 t. dried oregano
1/4 t. cayenne pepper
1 t. salt
1/2 t. pepper
15-oz. can ranch-style beans

In a large skillet over medium heat, brown beef with onion and green pepper; drain. Add remaining ingredients except beans; stir well. Reduce heat to medium-low. Simmer for 30 minutes to one hour, stirring occasionally. Add beans and heat through. Makes 4 servings.

There's no such thing as too much chili! Freeze leftovers in small containers, to be reheated and spooned over hot dogs or baked potatoes for a quick & hearty lunch.

Mother's Chili Soup

Carol Heard
Blue Lake, CA

This recipe was my mother's. It's great comfort food in the wintertime.
Once, I prepared this chili and served it in individual bread bowls.
My grandson loved it...he ate the soup, bread and all!

1 lb. ground beef
1/2 c. onion, chopped
garlic powder, salt and pepper
   to taste
1-1/4 oz. pkg. chili seasoning
   mix

2 to 3 8-oz. cans tomato sauce
2 to 3 15-1/2 oz. cans red
   kidney beans
Optional: 14-1/2 oz. can stewed
   tomatoes, chopped

In a soup pot over medium heat, brown beef with onion; drain. Add seasonings to taste. Stir in remaining ingredients. Reduce heat to medium-low. Simmer for 20 to 30 minutes, stirring occasionally. If desired, add a little water to desired thickness. Serves 4 to 6.

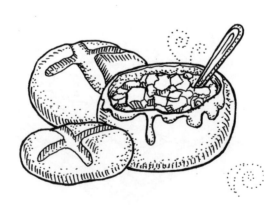

Bread bowls make hearty soup extra special. Cut the tops off round
loaves of bread and hollow out, then rub with olive oil and garlic.
Pop bread bowls in the oven at 400 degrees for 10 minutes,
or until crusty and golden. Ladle in soup and enjoy!

Chill-Chasing
Soups & Breads

Fast Fiesta Soup

Vickie
Gooseberry Patch

*Grandma always kept the cans in the cupboard in case we stopped at
her house for lunch. We loved her spicy meatless soup, especially if
there were corn chips on the side.*

2 10-oz. cans diced tomatoes &
   green chiles
15-1/2 oz. can black beans,
   drained and rinsed

15-1/4 oz. can corn, drained
Garnish: shredded Cheddar
   cheese, sour cream

In a saucepan over medium heat, combine tomatoes with juice, beans
and corn. Cook until bubbly and heated through. Garnish as desired.
Makes 4 servings.

Cheesy Bread Puffs

Joan Chance
Houston, TX

*I love to eat these delicious puffs with soup or salad. They freeze
very well, should you have extras.*

2 5-oz. jars sharp pasteurized
   process cheese spread
1/2 c. plus 2 T. butter, melted

1 egg, beaten
1 uncut loaf white bread, cut
   into 1-inch cubes

Mix together cheese, butter and egg until smooth. Dip bread cubes into
mixture, coating well. Arrange cubes on a lightly greased baking sheet;
cover and refrigerate overnight. To serve, bake at 400 degrees for
10 minutes, or until lightly golden. Serves 6 to 8.

Need to add a little zing to a soup or stew? Just add a
dash of herb-flavored vinegar...a super use for that
bottle you brought home from the farmers' market.

Grandma's Irish Stew

Helen Adams
Mabank, TX

This is a rustic stew that really sticks to your ribs and is just packed with flavor. It's the same stew that I had in Grandma's kitchen so many times when I was young. My grandma was Irish, and her heritage certainly came out in her cooking. This has brought back so many wonderful memories! Serve hot with Irish soda bread.

6 potatoes, peeled and cut into
   medium chunks
3 c. carrots, peeled and cut into
   1/2-inch chunks
2 yellow onions, coarsely
   chopped
4 stalks celery, chopped
3 cloves garlic, chopped
salt and pepper to taste

1/4 c. all-purpose flour
2 lbs. boneless beef or lamb,
   cut into 1-1/2 inch cubes
3 T. olive oil
3 c. beef broth
12-oz. bottle Irish stout beer,
   or 12-oz. can cola
1 T. dried thyme
1 T. dried parsley

Combine vegetables and garlic in a large bowl. Season generously with salt and pepper. Sprinkle with flour; toss until well coated. In a separate bowl, season beef or lamb cubes with salt and pepper; set aside. Heat oil in a very heavy Dutch oven over medium-high heat. Add meat cubes; cook until well browned on all sides. Add vegetables; mix well. Stir in broth and beer or cola. Bring to a boil; reduce heat to medium-low. Simmer for 2 hours, stirring occasionally. Add seasonings; continue cooking over low heat for another 30 minutes to one hour. Makes 8 servings.

What good fortune to grow up in a home
where there are grandparents.
– Suzanne LaFollette

Chill-Chasing
Soups & Breads

Irish Soda Bread

Barbara Holland Kelly
Liberty, NY

This is my family's recipe for Irish soda bread from my grandmother, who came from County Cork, Ireland. Everyone who tries it loves it. No other can compare. Sláinte...to your health!

3-1/2 c. all-purpose flour, divided	3 T. butter
1/3 c. sugar	1 c. raisins
1/2 t. baking powder	1 T. caraway seed
1 t. baking soda	2 eggs, beaten
	2 c. buttermilk

In a large bowl, combine 3-1/4 cups flour, sugar, baking powder and baking soda; mix well. Cut in butter with a fork until mixture looks like cornmeal. Add raisins and caraway seed. Whisk eggs and buttermilk in a small bowl; add gradually to flour mixture. Mix well for one minute. Dough will be moist. Sprinkle some of remaining flour in an ungreased cast-iron skillet; pat in dough to fill pan. (A 9"x5" loaf pan may also be used.) Dip a knife into flour and cut a criss-cross in the center of dough. Sprinkle a little flour over all. Bake at 425 degrees for 35 to 40 minutes. Cool before slicing. Makes one loaf.

A single vintage quilt patch makes a charming topper for a bread basket. Just stitch it to a large napkin in a matching color.

Potato & Sausage Chowder

Wendy Meadows
Spring Hill, FL

After my grandmother passed away, I found this recipe
in her recipe box. It was her mother's recipe that
has now been handed down to me.

2 c. potatoes, peeled and diced
1/2 c. carrots, peeled and diced
1/2 c. celery, diced
1/4 c. onion, chopped
1 t. salt
8 c. low-sodium chicken or
   vegetable broth
5 links sweet or hot Italian
   pork sausage

1/4 c. butter
1/4 c. all-purpose flour
2 c. milk
12-oz. pkg. frozen corn, thawed
12-oz. pkg. frozen cut green
   beans, thawed
2-1/2 c. shredded Cheddar
   cheese

Combine potatoes, carrots, celery, onion and salt in a large soup pot;
add broth to cover. Bring to a boil over high heat. Reduce heat to
medium and simmer for 20 minutes. While soup simmers, place sausage
links in a skillet; add enough water to come up halfway. Simmer over
medium-high heat for 8 to 10 minutes, turning often. Remove sausages
to a cutting board; let cool slightly and slice into rounds. Add sausage
to simmering soup. In a small saucepan over medium-low heat, blend
butter and flour; add milk. Cook, stirring constantly, until smooth and
thick. Add milk mixture to soup; continue simmering until thickened.
Stir in corn and beans; simmer until tender. Add cheese; cook and stir
until melted. Makes 8 servings.

Evaporated milk was a standby in Grandma's day. It's still handy
because it's extra creamy and needs no refrigeration. Keep several cans
in the pantry to use in soups and gravies that call for regular milk.

Chill-Chasing
Soups & Breads

Easy Cheesy Potato Soup

Dana Rowan
Spokane, WA

This recipe has been handed down through my family for years. My Aunt Barb always made it, and it was so good, especially on a cold day. It is gluten-free, which is hard to find in a creamy soup. Add some warm, crusty bread and you've got a satisfying meal!

2 c. potatoes, peeled and chopped
1/2 c. celery, finely diced
1/4 c. onion, chopped, or
    2 T. dried, minced onion
2 c. water
1/4 c. butter

2 c. pasteurized process cheese,
    diced
2 c. milk
1 c. cooked ham or bacon, diced
Garnish: shredded Cheddar
    cheese, crumbled bacon

In a soup pot, combine potatoes, celery, onion and water. Cook over medium heat for 20 minutes. Stir in remaining ingredients except garnish. Cook, stirring occasionally, until butter and cheese are melted and all ingredients are combined. Top each bowl with Cheddar cheese and bacon. Serves 8 to 10.

At farmers' markets and even at the supermarket, watch for heirloom vegetables...varieties that Grandma might have grown in her garden. These veggies don't always look picture-perfect, but their flavor can't be beat!

Grandma's Favorites

Hearty Split Pea Soup

Erin Brock
Charleston, WV

Years ago, my grandma used to make split pea soup in a big black cast-iron kettle. I loved it, but never got the recipe. Recently I've been trying to duplicate her soup...I think this is finally it!

16-oz. pkg. dried split peas
8 c. low-sodium chicken broth
2 potatoes, peeled and diced
2 onions, diced
2 carrots, peeled and diced
1/2 c. celery, chopped

2 c. cooked ham, diced
1 t. dried marjoram
1 t. poultry seasoning
1 t. dried sage
salt and pepper to taste

Combine all ingredients in a Dutch oven; stir well. Bring to a boil over medium heat; reduce heat to medium-low. Cover and simmer for one hour and 15 minutes, stirring occasionally, until vegetables are tender. Makes 8 to 10 servings.

Country Zucchini Bread

Debbie McMurry
Pittsburg, KS

I have fond memories of my grandmother baking this yummy bread for us every summer.

3 eggs, beaten
1-1/4 c. sugar
1 c. oil
2 c. all-purpose flour
1/4 t. baking powder
2 t. baking soda

1 T. cinnamon
2 t. nutmeg
1 t. salt
2 t. vanilla extract
2 c. zucchini, shredded
1 c. chopped pecans

In a large bowl, mix all ingredients in the order given. Pour batter into a greased and floured 9"x5" loaf pan. Bake at 350 degrees for 45 minutes. Cool loaf on a wire rack. Makes one loaf.

For the best flavor, crush dried herbs in your hand before adding them to a kettle of hot soup.

Chill-Chasing
Soups & Breads

Homemade Vegetable Soup

Carolyn Long
Wright City, MO

Growing up, I always loved my mother's vegetable soup. When I got married in 1967, I decided I would carry on the recipe in my family. Now we have two sons who are married with three grandchildren. I've added a few different things to my own veggie soup, and my family loves it. Fresh-baked bread goes very well with this soup.

2 32-oz. cans cocktail vegetable
    juice
1 lb. beef sirloin steak, cubed
1/2 head cabbage, coarsely
    chopped
8 carrots, peeled and thinly sliced
3/4 c. onion, finely chopped

3 14-1/2 oz. cans cut green
    beans, drained
12-oz. pkg. frozen corn
12-oz. frozen peas
2 t. salt
coarse pepper to taste

Add all ingredients to a large stew pot; stir well. Bring to a boil over medium-high heat; reduce heat to low. Simmer for about 1-1/2 hours, stirring occasionally. Season with additional salt and pepper, if desired. Makes 8 to 10 servings.

Soup is so nice when shared. Thank a friend with a basket of
warm rolls and a pot of steaming homemade soup.

Dutch Oven Beef Stew

Glorya Hendrickson
Hesperia, CA

My family loves this stew. It's especially good during cold weather! It's very filling, and the house smells wonderful while it's cooking.

2 lbs. stew beef cubes
1 T. canola oil
2 c. hot water
1 medium onion, sliced
1 clove garlic
1 t. Worcestershire sauce
1 bay leaf
1 t. sugar
1/8 t. ground cloves

1 T. salt
1/4 t. pepper
4 potatoes, peeled and cut into
 large cubes
6 carrots, peeled and sliced
 1/2-inch thick
1 large onion, quartered
1/3 c. cold water
3 T. all-purpose flour

In a non-stick Dutch oven over medium-high heat, brown beef cubes in oil on all sides. Add hot water, sliced onion, garlic, Worcestershire sauce, bay leaf and seasonings. Bring to a boil over high heat; reduce heat to medium-low. Cover and simmer for 1-1/2 hours, stirring occasionally. Remove bay leaf and garlic; add potatoes, carrots and quartered onion. Cover and simmer for 45 minutes, or until vegetables are tender. In a cup, slowly blend cold water into flour. Stir mixture slowly into hot stew. Cook and stir until bubbly; cook for 3 minutes longer, or until thickened. Makes 6 to 8 servings.

A toasty touch for soups! Butter bread slices and cut into shapes using mini cookie cutters. Bake at 425 degrees for a few minutes, until crisp and golden. Place atop filled soup bowls at serving time.

Mom's Buttermilk Biscuits

LaDeana Cooper
Batavia, OH

*I can remember waking up to the smell of fresh biscuits in the oven.
Even now, whenever I make them, I am magically transported
back to my childhood.*

3 c. self-rising flour
1 c. cold butter, sliced

1 c. buttermilk
Optional: melted butter

Add flour to a large bowl. Cut in butter with 2 knives until mixture
resembles coarse meal. Slowly stir in buttermilk until a soft dough ball
forms. Dough will be sticky. Turn dough out onto a lightly floured
surface; fold about 15 to 20 times. Roll out dough, one to 1-1/2 inches
thick. Cut with a 2 to 3-inch round biscuit cutter or a glass tumbler.
Place biscuits on ungreased baking sheets. Bake at 350 degrees for
20 minutes, or until lightly golden. Brush tops with melted butter, if
desired. Makes 1-1/2 to 2 dozen biscuits.

Make your own self-rising flour! Combine one cup all-purpose flour,
1/2 teaspoon salt and 1-1/2 teaspoons baking powder. This equals
one cup self-rising flour.

Creamy Shrimp Chowder

Darrell Lawry
Kissimmee, FL

Grandma's specialty...a simple and elegant soup. Sometimes she adds a half-cup of sweet corn for color and flavor.

1/2 c. celery, chopped
1/3 c. onion, diced
2 T. butter
1 c. milk
8-oz. pkg. cream cheese, cubed

1-1/2 c. cooked potatoes, diced
1/2 lb. cooked small shrimp,
    thawed and drained if frozen
2 T. white wine or water
1/2 t. salt

In a large saucepan over medium heat, sauté celery and onion in butter. Add milk and cheese; cook and stir over low heat until cheese melts. Add potatoes, shrimp, wine or water and salt. Heat through over low heat, stirring occasionally. Makes 6 servings.

Simple Drop Biscuits

Lisa Ann Panzino DiNunzio
Vineland, NJ

These yummy biscuits are simple to make and complement any meal. Just watch how fast they disappear!

2 c. all-purpose flour
1 T. baking powder
2 t. sugar
1/2 t. cream of tartar

1/4 t. salt
1/2 c. butter, melted
1 c. milk

In a large bowl, combine flour, baking powder, sugar, cream of tartar and salt. Stir in butter and milk just until moistened. Drop batter by tablespoonfuls onto a lightly greased baking sheet. Bake at 450 degrees for 8 to 12 minutes, until golden around the edges. Serve warm. Makes 8 to 10 biscuits.

Next time the soup boils over onto the stovetop, cover cooked-on food spots with equal parts baking soda and water. Spills will soak right off.

New England Clam Chowder

Robin Hill
Rochester, NY

My grandmother made delicious clam chowder the old-fashioned way, using clams in the shell and salt pork. We all loved it, but it was quite a production to make it. This recipe brings back memories of eating Grandma's chowder without all of the effort.

3 6-oz. cans chopped clams,
    drained and liquid reserved
1/4 lb. bacon, diced
2 onions, chopped
2 T. all-purpose flour
3 c. potatoes, peeled and diced

1 T. celery flakes
2 t. salt
1/4 t. celery salt
1/4 t. pepper
3 c. whole milk
1 T. butter

Combine reserved clam liquid and enough water to equal 2 cups; set aside. In a soup pot over medium heat, cook bacon until nearly crisp. Add onions and sauté until tender, about 5 minutes. Sprinkle with flour; cook and stir until blended. Gradually stir in clam liquid. Cook, stirring constantly, until slightly thickened. Stir in potatoes and seasonings. Cover and cook until potatoes are tender, about 10 minutes. Add clams, milk and butter; cover and cook until heated through, about 5 minutes. Makes 6 servings.

Let the kids try their hand at making butter! Pour a pint of heavy cream into a chilled wide-mouth jar, cap the jar tightly and take turns shaking until you see butter begin to form. When it's done, rinse the butter lightly with cool water. Enjoy on warm, fresh-baked bread...yum!

Mom's Vegetable-Hamburger Soup

Evangeline Boston
Ellenton, FL

When I was growing up, we lived in a house built by my dad and his brother. It was so cold! Snow blew in the window cracks and piled on the floor. Only one black cookstove warmed the whole house. Mom made lots of pots of soups on that stove, cornbread and pies too. She made a soup like this, but I have made it easier for a quick dinner. You won't need to add any seasoning. Serve with chopped onions, shredded cheese and buttery cornbread...that's it!

1 to 1-1/2 lbs. lean ground beef
32-oz. can tomato juice
15-1/2 oz. can Great Northern
    beans, navy beans or black
    beans, or black-eyed peas
15-oz. can corn

15-oz. can green peas
15-oz. can diced potatoes
14-1/2 oz. can cut green beans
14-1/2 oz. can sliced carrots
Optional: 15-1/2 oz. can hominy

In a large stockpot over medium heat, cook beef until no longer pink. Do not drain. Add tomato juice and all cans of vegetables, undrained. Stir gently to mix. Simmer over medium-low heat for one hour, stirring occasionally and adding some water if a thinner consistency is desired. Makes 8 to 10 servings.

Stir some alphabet pasta into a pot of vegetable soup...
the kids will love it!

Great-Grandma Allen's Rolls

Lindsey Martinez
Grass Lake, MI

My grandma and I used to make these rolls every year for Thanksgiving. It was something special that I looked forward to. Now that I am all grown up, I get to make these for my own family!

2 c. milk
1/2 c. shortening
1 c. warm water, 110 to
    115 degrees
3/4 c. sugar
2 envs. quick-rise yeast

1 T. salt
5 to 8 c. all-purpose flour,
    divided
2 eggs, beaten
Garnish: melted butter

Add milk to a saucepan over medium-low heat; bring almost to a boil. Add shortening; stir once or twice, until melted. Add warm water. Allow mixture to cool down to 128 to 130 degrees. Meanwhile, in a large bowl, combine sugar, yeast, salt and 5 cups flour; stir well. Add milk mixture; beat with an electric mixer on medium speed until mixed well. Add eggs; beat well. Continue to beat in remaining flour, a little at a time, until a smooth dough ball forms. Dough should not be too dry. If too difficult to beat dough with mixer, knead with your hands until smooth. Lightly grease a large bowl with shortening; turn dough ball in bowl to coat. Cover with a tea towel and set in a warm spot for about one hour, until risen. Divide dough into half. On a floured surface, roll out each half to 1/2-inch thick. Cut into circles with a 2-1/2 inch biscuit cutter or glass tumbler. Crease in the center with a knife; brush with butter. Arrange rolls on baking sheets sprayed with non-stick vegetable spray. Cover and let rise again for about one hour. Bake at 400 degrees for 15 to 20 minutes, until golden. Makes about 4 dozen.

When baking bread, if the water added to yeast is too hot, it will kill the yeast. Use Grandma's old trick to test the temperature... sprinkle the heated water on your forearm. If it doesn't feel either hot or cold, the temperature is just right for the yeast.

Grandma's Chicken-Corn Soup & Rivels

Heather Strauss
Waynesboro, PA

This was one of the first recipes that my grandma taught me to cook. She was one of the best cooks I know, so I was excited when she said she would write it down and teach me. Most of her recipes were still in her head, so this was a treat. It makes enough to feed an army, and is so worth it!

3 to 4-lb. roasting chicken
Optional: 1 to 2 14-oz. cans
   chicken broth
16 c. water
3 to 4 T. chicken soup base

1 c. onion, chopped
2 stalks celery, chopped
12 c. fresh or frozen corn
salt and pepper to taste

Place chicken in a roasting pan; cover with water almost to the top. Cover and bake at 350 degrees for about 2 hours, until very tender. Remove chicken to a platter to cool. Measure out 12 cups of broth from roasting pan into a very large stockpot. If needed, add canned broth to equal 12 cups broth. Add 16 cups water, soup base, vegetables and seasonings to stockpot. Bring to a boil over medium heat; simmer for 20 minutes. Shred chicken and add to simmering broth. Slowly add crumbled Rivels dough, stirring constantly, until all the dough is in the stockpot. Simmer soup for about 20 minutes more, stirring occasionally, until rivels are cooked through. Season to taste with more salt and pepper, as desired. Makes 15 to 20 servings.

Rivels:

3 to 4 c. all-purpose flour
1/2 t. salt

4 eggs

In a large bowl, mix 3 cups flour and salt; make a well in the center. Add eggs to well. Using your hands, blend eggs into flour mixture until mixture sticks together but is still crumbly, adding more flour as needed.

Chill-Chasing
Soups & Breads

Chicken & Wild Rice Soup

Claudia Keller
Carrollton, GA

My great-aunt lives in Minnesota. Every Christmas, she sends us a gift basket with a packet of wild rice. When I asked her how she likes to cook it, she shared this tasty, easy recipe with me.

3 14-oz. cans chicken broth, divided
1/2 c. wild rice, uncooked and rinsed
1 c. carrot, peeled and coarsely chopped
1/2 c. celery, chopped
1/2 c. onion, chopped

2 c. sliced mushrooms
2 T. butter
1/4 c. all-purpose flour
1/4 t. salt
1/4 t. pepper
8-oz. container whipping cream
2 c. cooked chicken breast, diced

In a soup pot, combine 2 cans broth, uncooked rice, carrot, celery and onion. Bring to a boil over medium-high heat; reduce heat to medium-low. Cover and simmer for 30 to 35 minutes, stirring occasionally, just until rice is tender. Add mushrooms; cook another 5 minutes. Meanwhile, in a separate saucepan, melt butter over medium heat. Stir in flour, salt and pepper; add remaining broth. Cook and stir until thickened and bubbly; cook and stir for one more minute. Stir in cream. Add cream mixture to rice mixture, stirring constantly over low heat until blended. Stir in chicken; heat through. Makes 8 servings.

If a pot of soup starts to burn on the bottom, don't worry. Spoon it into another pan, being careful not to scrape up the scorched bits on the bottom. The burnt taste usually won't linger.

61

Creamy Chicken & Shells Soup

Carolyn Deckard
Bedford, IN

This was my mom's busy-day soup...we had it for lunch and supper. It's still one of my favorites and always reminds me how good Mom's cooking was.

3 to 4 pieces chicken
4 c. water
1 c. onion, diced
1/4 c. celery, chopped
1/4 c. fresh parsley, minced, or 1 T. dried parsley
1 bay leaf
1 t. salt
1/4 t. white pepper
2 c. medium shell macaroni, uncooked

2 to 3 potatoes, peeled and diced
4 to 5 green onions, chopped
3 cubes chicken bouillon
1/2 t. seasoned salt
1/2 t. poultry seasoning
4 c. milk
1/4 c. butter
1/4 c. all-purpose flour
Garnish: nutmeg, additional parsley

In a Dutch oven, combine chicken, water, onion, celery, parsley, bay leaf, salt and pepper. Simmer over medium heat until chicken is tender, 20 to 25 minutes. Meanwhile, cook macaroni as package directions; drain and set aside. Remove chicken to a plate to cool; reserve broth in pan. Coarsely chop chicken; discard skin and bones and set aside. Discard bay leaf. Add potatoes, onions, bouillon cubes and seasonings to broth. Simmer for 15 minutes. Return chicken to pan; add milk and macaroni. Return to a simmer. Melt butter over medium heat in a small saucepan. Add flour to butter; cook, stirring constantly, until mixture begins to brown. Add to soup; blend well. Cover and let soup stand for 20 minutes to blend flavors. Season to taste. Garnish with nutmeg and parsley. Makes 8 servings.

Keep your salt shaker free-flowing in summer humidity. Just add 5 or 10 grains of rice to the shaker.

Chill-Chasing
Soups & Breads

Grandma's Turkey Soup

*Kathie Craig
Burlington, WI*

Do you remember the turkey soup your grandma made after Thanksgiving? This is it! You can use up almost any leftover veggies...peas, beans, collard greens, broccoli, etc.

1 meaty turkey frame
8 c. water
3/4 c. onion, finely chopped
1 t. Worcestershire sauce
1/2 t. dried sage
1 bay leaf
1-1/2 c. corn

1 c. celery, chopped, with some
   leaves included
1 c. carrots, peeled and shredded
2 T. fresh parsley, snipped,
   or 1 t. dried parsley
salt and pepper to taste

Break turkey frame to fit a large soup pot. Add water, onion, Worcestershire sauce, sage and bay leaf. Bring to a boil over high heat; reduce heat to medium-low. Cover and simmer for 1-1/2 hours. Remove turkey frame and let cool. Add vegetables and parsley to soup. Dice turkey when cooled; add to soup pot. Cover and simmer for 45 minutes, stirring occasionally. Discard bay leaf. Season to taste with salt and pepper. Makes 8 to 10 servings.

Keep a bag of frozen peas in the freezer in case of bumps and boo-boos. It will conform safely and easily to a knee or elbow. When the tears have stopped and the peas are thawed, just toss them into a soup pot or casserole. A time-honored tradition that's still handy!

Grandma's Brown Bread

Denise Thompson
Bridgeton, NJ

This recipe has been handed down from my grandmother to my mother and on to me. I have passed it along to my daughters, so you know it's special! It's a little unusual in that it cooks on the stovetop, not in the oven.

1 c. whole-wheat flour	1 c. cornmeal
1 c. graham flour	2 c. sour milk or buttermilk
1 t. baking soda	1/2 c. brown sugar, packed
1 t. salt	3/4 c. molasses

In a large bowl, mix together flours, baking soda and salt. Add remaining ingredients; mix well and set aside. Grease two 16-ounce cans; divide batter evenly between cans. Cover each can with a piece of aluminum foil. Set cans on a rack in a Dutch oven. Add 2 inches of water to pan. Place Dutch oven on the stovetop over medium-high heat; bring to a boil. Reduce heat to medium-low; simmer gently for 2-1/2 hours. Add more water as needed to prevent pan from boiling dry. When done, immediately run a table knife around the inside of each can and turn loaves out. Slice and serve. Makes 2 loaves.

If an old recipe calls for a cup of sour milk, just stir a teaspoon of white vinegar into a cup of fresh milk and let it stand for a few minutes. Buttermilk is a good substitute too.

Chill-Chasing
Soups & Breads

Mom's 2-Can Corn Chowder

Christine Beauregard
Keene, NH

My mom was always asked to bring her creamy corn chowder to our family gatherings. She's no longer able to cook, so now it's my turn to bring Mom's corn chowder...yum! Thanks, Mom.

1/2 c. butter
1 onion, chopped
2 15-oz. cans diced potatoes, drained
2 15-oz. cans corn, drained

2 14-3/4 oz. cans creamed corn
2 5-oz. cans evaporated milk
salt and pepper to taste
Garnish: oyster crackers

Melt butter in a large saucepan over medium heat. Add onion; cook for 10 minutes, or until caramelized. Add potatoes, corn, creamed corn and evaporated milk; stir well. Cook, stirring often, over medium-low heat for 15 minutes; do not allow to boil. Add salt and pepper to taste. Serve with oyster crackers. Makes 8 servings.

Make a simple herb wreath to enjoy. Cover a grapevine wreath with sprigs of fresh herbs like sage, rosemary and thyme...simply slip long stems into the wreath until it's covered. Hung in a warm kitchen, the herbs will dry naturally and can be enjoyed year 'round.

4-Ingredient Chicken Soup

Sharon Sayre
Sweet Valley, PA

A great soup for kids! Sometimes we watch our grandchildren. When they come through the door, they always say, "Mommy & Daddy didn't feed us, can we have your soup?" Of course I always make it! It's also great when you're not feeling well. For a heartier soup, add a drained can of sliced carrots or flaked chicken.

6 c. water
6-oz. pkg. pastina or acini de
   pepe pasta, uncooked

6 envs. instant chicken broth
2 T. grated Parmesan cheese

In a saucepan over high heat, bring water to a boil. Add pasta and broth; cook according to package directions. Do not drain. Sprinkle with cheese just before serving. Makes 6 servings.

It's fine to keep a few days' worth of butter on the countertop in a covered crock. It'll be soft and spreadable anytime, ready for spreading on rolls or bread.

Fresh-Picked from
Grandma's Garden

Veggie-Loaded Family Potato Salad

Judy Loemker
Edwardsville, IL

I've been fixing this recipe for the past 43 years, ever since I married the love of my life. There are only two potato salad recipes we really enjoy...this one, and my family's German potato salad recipe. This is a "lighter" potato salad, using four other vegetables in addition to the potatoes. The dressing is also one of my favorites. I hope you enjoy it as much as we do!

8 redskin or Yukon Gold potatoes
1-1/2 c. celery, sliced
1 c. radishes, thinly sliced
1-1/4 c. green onions, sliced
1-1/3 c. cucumber, cubed
2 c. regular or light mayonnaise

2 T. mustard
4 to 5 t. lemon juice
1 t. celery seed
2 t. seasoned salt
pepper to taste

In a large saucepan, cover whole, unpeeled potatoes with salted water. Bring to a boil over high heat; reduce heat to medium. Cook until fork-tender, about 35 to 40 minutes. Drain. Cool potatoes slightly; peel if desired and cut into cubes. In a large bowl, combine potatoes with celery, radishes, onions and cucumber. In a separate bowl, mix remaining ingredients; spoon over vegetables and toss to coat well. Cover and chill before serving. Makes 8 to 10 servings.

Speedy salad topper! An egg slicer makes short work of slicing mushrooms and olives as well as hard-boiled eggs. Works great on strawberries and bananas too.

Fresh-Picked from
Grandma's Garden

Aunt Vernie's Home-Grown Garden Salad

Sandy Coffey
Cincinnati, OH

As a child, I used to spend summers in West Virginia, and all the ingredients for a delicious fresh-from-the-garden summer salad were right outside, in the garden. Great memories!

1 head lettuce, torn
4 stalks celery, sliced
2 onions, chopped
2 tomatoes, chopped
1 green or red pepper, chopped

1 carrot, peeled and shredded
1 cucumber, peeled and chopped
5 radishes, thinly sliced
favorite salad dressing to taste
shredded Colby cheese to taste

Combine all vegetables in a large bowl; toss to mix. Add desired amount of salad dressing; mix well. Top with shredded cheese. Cover and chill, if not serving immediately. Makes 6 to 8 servings.

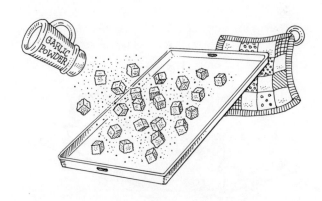

Savory homemade croutons are easy to make. Toss cubes of day-old bread with olive oil, garlic powder, salt and pepper. Place bread cubes in a single layer on a baking sheet and bake at 400 degrees for about 10 minutes, until toasty.

Vegetable Marinade

Sharon Lundberg
Longwood, FL

My mom would make this cool salad dish to take to a potluck or serve during a special occasion. It is nice to take to a potluck because it's made ahead, then served chilled. Just set it on the table and no worries about keeping it warm.

4 stalks celery, chopped
1 c. canned diced pimentos,
   drained
1/2 c. red onion, chopped
1/3 c. green pepper, chopped
14-1/2 oz. can French-style
   green beans, drained

15-oz. can petite green peas,
   drained
1 c. olive oil, or to taste
1/2 c. red wine vinegar
1/2 c. sugar
1 t. paprika
1 t. salt

In a large bowl, combine celery, pimentos, onion and green pepper; toss to mix. Add beans and peas; mix gently. Add remaining ingredients; stir well. Cover and chill for 24 hours. Use a slotted spoon to drain slightly before serving. Makes 6 to 8 servings.

Spoon servings of pasta salad into hollowed-out tomato halves...
so pretty on the dining table!

Fresh-Picked from
Grandma's Garden

Fresh Cucumber Salad

Angie Stone
Argillite, KY

My grandmother made this tasty salad for my husband so often through the years. She could hardly wait for the fresh cucumbers to be ready in our garden so she could create this salad.

7 c. cucumbers, sliced
1 c. red onion, sliced
1 c. red pepper, sliced
1 c. vinegar

2 c. sugar
1 t. celery seed
1 t. mustard seed
1 T. salt

Layer cucumbers, onion and pepper in a 2-quart bowl; set aside. In a saucepan over medium heat, combine remaining ingredients. Bring to a boil; cook and stir until sugar dissolves. Allow to cool. Pour cooled vinegar mixture over vegetables; toss to mix. Cover and chill 24 hours before serving. Makes 12 to 16 servings.

Tomato-Mozzarella Salad

Joanna Nicoline-Haughey
Berwyn, PA

I remember Mom serving this simple salad in the summertime, made with fresh ingredients from Dad's wonderful garden full of sun-ripe tomatoes, cucumbers, green peppers and herbs. What great memories!

4 tomatoes, cubed
1 cucumber, sliced
1 c. part-skim mozzarella cheese,
   cubed

1 T. fresh basil, chopped
2 T. canola oil
1/4 t. pepper

Mix tomatoes, cucumber, cheese and basil in a serving bowl. Drizzle with oil and toss to mx; sprinkle with pepper. Makes 8 servings.

For fresh-from-the-garden taste, store ripe tomatoes stem-side down at room temperature, not in the refrigerator.

Refrigerator Carrot Salad

Sara Tatham
Plymouth, NH

This salad adds wonderful color and flavor to a buffet table! It's a combination of a recipe from our pastor's wife and one I found in a wonderful old cookbook. I've adjusted the quantities to make it lower in fat and sugar than either of the originals.

2 lbs. carrots, peeled and sliced into coins	3/4 c. vinegar
10-3/4 oz. can tomato soup	1 t. dry mustard
1/3 c. sugar	1 t. Worcestershire sauce
1/4 c. oil	1 to 2 T. dried, minced onion
	1 green pepper, sliced into strips

In a large saucepan, cover carrots with boiling salted water. Bring to a boil over high heat; reduce heat to medium. Cover and cook until crisp-tender, about 7 minutes; drain. In a bowl, blend together remaining ingredients except onion and green pepper; stir into carrots, coating well. Fold in onion and green pepper. Cover and refrigerate at least 4 hours before serving. May keep refrigerated up to 5 days. Makes 2 quarts, about 8 servings.

Celebrate Grandparents' Day, September 12, by inviting Grandma & Grandpa to Sunday dinner. Let them relax and take it easy while the rest of the family does all the cooking and serving!

Fresh-Picked from
Grandma's Garden

Mom's Coleslaw

Krista Marshall
Fort Wayne, IN

My mom and grandma have been making this very simple coleslaw for years, and to this day, it's still my favorite kind. Mom always used her favorite mayonnaise-type salad dressing, never mayo.

1 head cabbage, shredded
3/4 c. mayonnaise-type salad
   dressing
1 T. dried parsley

1-1/2 t. cider vinegar
1 t. sugar
salt and pepper to taste
paprika to taste

Place cabbage in a large bowl. In another bowl, combine remaining ingredients except paprika; mix until smooth. Spoon mixture over cabbage; toss until well blended. Sprinkle with paprika. Cover and chill until serving. Makes 6 servings.

Great-Aunt's Broccoli-Cauliflower Salad

Renee Johnson
Cookeville, TN

This recipe was given to me by my Great-Aunt Elizabeth. She was my grandmother's sister, and they were both wonderful cooks. This is a good dish to take to potlucks.

1 c. mayonnaise-type salad
   dressing
1/2 c. sour cream
1 T. sugar
1 T. vinegar

5 c. broccoli flowerets
2-1/2 c. cauliflower flowerets
1 c. onion, chopped
2 c. cherry tomatoes

Combine salad dressing, sour cream, sugar and vinegar; stir well. Cover and chill for 6 hours. At serving time, combine vegetables in a large bowl. Pour dressing mixture over vegetables and mix well. Makes 8 servings.

For a yummy change of pace, stir pineapple tidbits, mandarin oranges or chopped apple into sweet, creamy coleslaw.

Rainbow Pasta Salad

LaShelle Brown
Mulvane, KS

This is my husband's all-time favorite pasta salad. He requests it at all of our summer events. Add cubes of ham or salami for an eaven heartier salad.

4 c. rainbow rotini pasta,
   uncooked
1 cucumber, quartered
   lengthwise and sliced
1 tomato, chopped
4-oz. can sliced black olives,
   drained

1 c. ranch salad dressing
1/3 c. Italian salad dressing
Garnish: shredded sharp
   Cheddar cheese

Cook pasta according to package directions; drain and rinse with cold water. In a large salad bowl, combine cooked pasta, cucumber, tomato and olives; mix well. In a separate bowl, mix salad dressings together. Add to pasta mixture; toss to coat. Cover and refrigerate for at least one hour. Just before serving, sprinkle with shredded cheese. Serves 8.

Whip up some homemade buttermilk dressing...wonderful on tossed salads and a delicious dip for fresh veggies too. Blend 1/2 cup buttermilk, 1/2 cup mayonnaise, one teaspoon dried parsley, 1/2 teaspoon onion powder, 1/4 teaspoon garlic powder, 1/8 teaspoon dill weed and a little salt and pepper. Keep refrigerated.

Fresh-Picked from
Grandma's Garden

Mom's Pick-of-the-Crop Tomato Salad

Lillian Child
Omaha, NE

My mom loved making plain old tomato sandwiches for us kids with homemade bread, sliced ripe tomatoes and mayonnaise when tomatoes were plentiful, and boy, were they good! She also made this wonderful tomato salad that I now make for my family. They request it often, especially when tomatoes are at their finest in August! Enjoy it as a wonderful refreshing side dish to anything off the grill.

4 to 6 ripe beefsteak tomatoes,
   quartered
1 cucumber, peeled and cubed
1 red onion, sliced into rings
4 eggs, hard-boiled and sliced,
   whites only

1 c. ranch salad dressing,
   or to taste
2 t. fresh dill weed, snipped
1/2 t. pepper
Optional: 4 to 6 slices bacon,
   crisply cooked and crumbled

Combine all ingredients in a large bowl; mix gently. Cover and refrigerate for about an hour, so that flavors can blend. Stir well before serving. Makes 6 to 8 servings.

Fill a canister with vintage green-handled kitchen utensils to set on the kitchen counter...instant nostalgia!

Mama's Ambrosia

Sue Morrison
Blue Springs, MO

My mama, and her mother before her, made this wonderful holiday salad. It is quick & easy with wonderful flavor and color. Mama always served this salad in a crystal bowl. I enjoy using my Fiestaware® bowl for a more casual meal. It is delicious with roast turkey, baked ham or chicken & dumplings. The perfect salad for a hungry family!

15-oz. can fruit cocktail
8-oz. can pineapple tidbits,
   drained
1 ripe banana, sliced
1/2 c. flaked coconut

1/2 c. mini marshmallows
1/2 c. chopped pecans
1 apple, cored and chopped
1 orange, sliced into small pieces
Optional: maraschino cherries

Combine fruit cocktail with juice, pineapple, banana, coconut, marshmallows and pecans. Toss gently so as not to mash banana. Fold in apple, orange and cherries, if using. Cover and refrigerate until ready to serve. Makes 8 servings.

Orange Sherbet Set Salad

Jill Ball
Highland, UT

My grandma was famous for her set salads, what we call a gelatin salad today. Every meal included at least one. Enjoy!

2 6-oz. pkgs. orange gelatin mix
4 c. boiling water
1 qt. orange sherbet, softened

2 11-oz. cans mandarin oranges,
   drained
3 ripe bananas, sliced

In a 13"x9" glass baking pan, combine gelatin mix and boiling water; stir until dissolved. Add sherbet and fruit; mix. Cover and chill until set. Makes 8 to 10 servings.

Sprinkle apple slices with a little lemon juice and they won't turn brown.

Fresh-Picked from
Grandma's Garden

Giddy-Up Grape Salad

Lori Peterson
Effingham, KS

My Aunt Betty brought this dish to a family dinner several years ago,
and I couldn't get enough. It's so simple, yet delicious!

8-oz. pkg. cream cheese,
  softened
1/2 c. sugar

3 lbs. seedless red grapes
1/4 c. brown sugar, packed
1/2 c. chopped pecans

In a large bowl, blend together cream cheese and sugar. Add grapes;
toss to mix gently. Spread into an 8"x8" baking pan and refrigerate. In a
small bowl, combine brown sugar and nuts; spread mixture on a baking
sheet. Bake at 350 degrees for 5 to 10 minutes, watching carefully,
until nuts are toasted. Stir; sprinkle mixture over salad. Cover and chill.
Serves 8 to 10.

Spiced Peaches

Betty Baehr
Kingsburg, CA

I grew up on these delicious peaches...my family grew peaches for
50 years! So good. The leftover syrup may be combined with
another can of drained peach halves.

13-oz. can peach halves, drained
1-qt. canning jar and lid,
  sterilized
1-1/2 c. honey

1/2 c. vinegar
3 3-inch cinnamon sticks
3 whole cloves

Arrange peach halves in canning jar; set aside. In a small saucepan over
low heat, bring remaining ingredients to a boil; pour over peaches and
cool. Cover and refrigerate for 8 hours before serving. Serves 4.

Pick up a vintage divided serving dish or two...
they're just right for serving up a choice of
veggie sides without crowding the table.

Grandma's German Potato Salad

Joyce Borrill
Utica, NY

Our fourth-generation specialty. Over the years, I'd watch Grandma add "little bits of this" and "little bits of that." Now that I've mastered those bits, I'm ready to share this recipe with so many others. It's a true family treasure, as was Grandma! This potato salad is great for family reunions, as I well know. It's always requested by many.

5 lbs. small white potatoes,
    uniformly sized
1-1/2 lbs. bacon, diced
3 sweet onions, sliced

1-1/4 c. white vinegar
3/4 c. sugar
2 t. salt
4 t. pepper

In a large Dutch oven, cover whole, unpeeled potatoes with water. Bring to a boil over high heat; reduce heat to medium. Cook until firm-tender, about 20 minutes. Drain and cool; refrigerate overnight. In the morning, cook bacon in a large skillet over medium heat until crisp; reduce heat to low. Peel potatoes and slice 1/4-inch thick; place in a large saucepan. Add remaining ingredients to potatoes. Toss gently over low heat until potatoes are warmed through. Add bacon with drippings to mixture. Toss potatoes for 5 to 7 minutes; do not stir. If too tart, add more sugar; if too sweet, add a little more vinegar. Serve warm. Makes 12 servings.

For potato salad, choose waxy new red, yellow or white potatoes.
They'll hold their shape much better than baking potatoes
when tossed with dressing.

Fresh-Picked from
Grandma's Garden

Italian Fried Green Tomatoes

Debra Elliott
Trussville, AL

*When I was growing up in the south, my grandma would always
cook sweet fried green tomatoes for Sunday supper, and their yummy
goodness melted in my mouth. This recipe is a sassy twist on my
grandma's recipe and is one of my family's favorite Sunday supper
side dishes.*

3 firm green tomatoes, each cut
    into 4 slices
1 to 2 c. all-purpose flour
1 T. garlic powder
1 t. dried oregano
2 eggs, beaten
2 c. buttermilk

2 c. Italian-seasoned dry bread
    crumbs
salt and pepper to taste
shortening or lard for frying
Garnish: chipotle mayonnaise,
    crumbled feta cheese

Place tomato slices in a bowl of ice water; set aside. In a shallow bowl,
combine flour and seasonings; mix well. In a separate shallow bowl,
whisk together eggs and buttermilk. Spread bread crumbs on a plate.
Drain tomatoes; pat dry with paper towels. Season both sides of tomato
slices with salt and pepper. Coat tomato slices with flour mixture; dip in
egg mixture. Coat with bread crumbs, pushing down to coat thoroughly.
Melt shortening or lard in a large cast-iron skillet over medium heat.
Add tomatoes to skillet, 4 slices at a time. Cook on each side until
fork-tender and golden. Remove to paper towels to drain. Drizzle slices
with chipotle mayonnaise; sprinkle with feta cheese. Serve warm.
Makes 4 to 8 servings.

Try just one herb at a time...a terrific way to learn which flavors you
like. Some tried & true pairs are ripe tomatoes and basil, sweet corn
and chives, cucumbers and mint, and potatoes and rosemary.

Marie's Herbed Spinach

Marie Fleetwood
Bloomington, IN

This recipe has been a favorite of mine and my family's for many years. In 1987, I entered it in a contest sponsored by our local newspaper...and won first prize in the vegetable category! Now I am 97 years old and don't do much cooking anymore, but I still enjoy reading cookbooks.

10-oz. pkg. frozen spinach,
   thawed and drained
1 c. long-cooking rice, cooked
1 c. shredded sharp Cheddar
   cheese
2 eggs, lightly beaten

2 T. butter, softened
1/3 c. whole milk
2 T. onion, chopped
1/2 t. Worcestershire sauce
1 t. salt
1/4 t. dried rosemary or thyme

In a large bowl, mix all ingredients together. Transfer to a greased 8"x8" baking pan. Bake, uncovered, at 350 degrees for 20 to 25 minutes. Makes 4 servings.

Garden-fresh vegetables are delicious steamed and topped with pats of chive butter. Blend 1/2 cup softened butter with 1/4 chopped fresh chives, 2 teaspoons lemon zest and a little salt & pepper. Pack into a crock and keep in the fridge...ready to use anytime.

Fresh-Picked from
Grandma's Garden

Catherine's Broccoli Casserole

*Cynthia Kimble
Lafayette, LA*

This recipe is from my mother, who was a sweet, funny lady. She was always in her kitchen, cooking for her family. She would make this dish for Christmas Eve dinner. She passed away a few years ago... miss you, Mom!

10-3/4 oz. can cream of
   mushroom soup
2/3 c. mayonnaise
1/4 c. onion, chopped
2 eggs, beaten

2 10-oz. pkgs. frozen chopped
   broccoli, cooked and well
   drained
1/4 c. butter, melted
3/4 c. soft bread crumbs

In a bowl, combine soup, mayonnaise and onion. Add eggs; mix well. Transfer mixture to a lightly greased 2-quart casserole dish. Add broccoli; stir to coat thoroughly. In a small bowl, toss together melted butter and bread crumbs; mix well and sprinkle over top. Bake, uncovered, at 350 degrees for 30 minutes, or until hot and bubbly. Makes 8 servings.

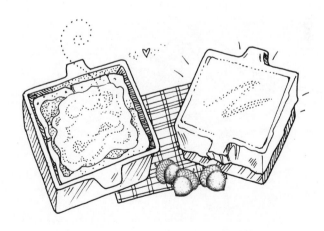

Enjoy a taste of summer in fall...make an extra of a favorite farm-fresh casserole to tuck into the freezer. Wrap well with plastic wrap and freeze. To serve, thaw overnight in the refrigerator and bake as usual.

Garden Vegetable Casserole

Linda Shively
Hopkinsville, KY

This recipe came from a friend of mine who always has a big garden. It is delicious, quick & easy.

2 yellow squash, sliced
1 zucchini, sliced
1 white onion, sliced
1 tomato, sliced
2 T. butter, melted

2 T. grated Parmesan cheese
1/2 t. dried basil
1/2 t. dried thyme
1/2 t. seasoned salt
garlic powder and pepper to taste

Combine vegetables in a lightly greased 2-quart casserole dish; mix gently. In a cup, combine melted butter, cheese and seasonings; mix well and drizzle over vegetables. Bake, uncovered, at 350 degrees for 45 minutes. Makes 6 servings.

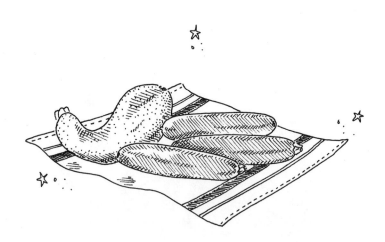

Zucchini and other summer squash make tasty side dishes and are easily swapped out in recipes. Try substituting old-fashioned yellow crookneck or pattypan squash for zucchini in any favorite recipe.

Fresh-Picked from
Grandma's Garden

Grandma Clarissa's Creamed Sweet Peas

Vickie Wiseman
Liberty Twp., OH

My grandmother would grow a garden every summer. She canned or
froze everything that she could. This is one of her recipes.

2 c. frozen peas, thawed
2/3 c. water
1/8 t. salt
3 T. butter, sliced

1/3 c. whipping cream
2 T. all-purpose flour
1 T. sugar

In a saucepan over medium-high heat, combine peas, water and salt.
Bring to a boil; reduce heat to low and stir in butter. In a small bowl,
whisk together remaining ingredients; stir into peas. Cook until mixture
thickens and bubbles, about 3 minutes; remove from heat. Sauce will
continue to thicken as it begins to cool. Serve while still warm. Makes
8 servings.

Mamaw's Skillet Cabbage

Beverley Williams
San Antonio, TX

This is the way my grandmother fixed cabbage. Cooking it
this way removes all the bitterness of the cabbage.

1 cabbage, chopped
2 c. milk

1/4 c. butter, thinly sliced
1 t. pepper, or to taste

Place cabbage in a large skillet. Add milk and enough water to nearly
fill the skillet. Dot with butter slices; sprinkle with pepper. Simmer over
medium-low heat for 30 minutes, stirring occasionally. Serve with a
slotted spoon to strain. Serves 6.

For bright color when cooking vegetables, add just a pinch of
baking soda to the water.

Tomatoes Piquant

Vickie Wiseman
Liberty Township, OH

This is a recipe that my mom used to make, using the fresh vegetables and herbs from her garden.

6 ripe tomatoes, peeled
2/3 c. olive oil
1/4 c. tarragon vinegar
1/4 c. green onions, sliced
1/4 c. fresh parsley, snipped
2 t. fresh thyme or marjoram,
   snipped

1 t. salt
1/4 t. pepper
1 clove garlic, minced
Garnish: additional snipped
   parsley

Place tomatoes in a deep bowl; set aside. Combine remaining ingredients except garnish in a jar; shake well and pour over tomatoes. Cover and chill for several hours or overnight, occasionally spooning dressing over tomatoes. At serving time, drain and discard dressing. Garnish tomatoes with additional parsley. Serves 8.

Peel tomatoes in a jiffy! Cut an "X" in the base of each tomato and place them in a deep saucepan. Carefully add boiling water to cover. After 20 to 30 seconds, remove the tomatoes with a slotted spoon and drop them into a bowl of ice water. The peels will slip right off.

Fresh-Picked from
Grandma's Garden

Mom's Eggplant Supreme

Jill Luffman
Mount Juliet, TN

*My mom has made this simple recipe for as long as I can remember.
It's wonderful in the summertime when veggies are fresh
from the garden or the farmers' market.*

2 eggplants, sliced 1-inch thick
2 to 3 tomatoes, sliced

1 sweet onion, thinly sliced
Garnish: chopped fresh basil

Arrange eggplant slices in a lightly greased 13"x9" glass baking pan.
Layer each eggplant slice with a tomato slice; layer each tomato slice
with several onion slices. Sprinkle with basil. Bake, uncovered, at
350 degrees for 25 to 30 minutes. Makes 8 servings.

Sliced eggplant tends to darken quickly. To keep it
light-colored, cook it right away or brush
with a little lemon juice.

Fresh Corn Fritters

Margaret Welder
Madrid, IA

This recipe came from my mother, so it is over 50 years old. It was a favorite of my children when they were growing up. The thyme and the Herb Mayonnaise are my additions. The mayonnaise is also delicious on sandwiches and salads, in deviled eggs or as a dip for fresh vegetables.

3 c. fresh or frozen corn
1/2 c. milk
2 eggs, beaten
2 T. butter, melted
3/4 c. all-purpose flour
1-1/2 t. baking powder

1 T. sugar
1 t. salt
1/4 t. pepper
1 T. fresh thyme, snipped
2 to 3 T. oil for frying

Thaw corn, if frozen. In a bowl, combine corn, milk, eggs and butter; stir well and set aside. In a separate bowl, combine remaining ingredients except oil. Add to corn mixture; stir just until combined. In a skillet over medium heat, heat one tablespoon oil until shimmering. Drop batter by heaping tablespoonfuls into hot oil. Cook, turning when fritters look crisp and begin to turn golden around the edges. Cook until no longer doughy in the center. Remove to a wire rack; keep warm while frying remaining batter, adding more oil as needed. Serve fritters with a dollop of Herb Mayonnaise. Serves 4 to 6.

Herb Mayonnaise:

1 c. mayonnaise
1 T. fresh flat-leaf Italian parsley,
    chopped
1 T. fresh chives, chopped

1-1/2 t. fresh basil, chopped
1-1/2 t. fresh dill weed, chopped
1-1/2 t. fresh oregano, chopped

Combine all ingredients; cover and keep refrigerated.

Chop fresh herbs in a jiffy...
use a pair of kitchen shears.

Fresh-Picked from
Grandma's Garden

Potato & Egg Casserole

Ginger Enright
Liberty, MO

This is a recipe that I remember my grandmother making often. She was an excellent cook! This dish goes wonderfully with ham.

6 eggs, hard-boiled
6 Yukon Gold potatoes
10-3/4 oz. can cream of chicken
   soup
8-oz. container sour cream
1/8 to 1/4 t. curry powder

1/4 t. salt
1/8 t. pepper
1/2 c. soft bread crumbs
2 to 3 T. butter, softened
1/2 c. shredded Cheddar cheese

Peel eggs and set aside. Cover potatoes with water in a saucepan. Cook over medium-high heat for 10 minutes; cool and peel. Meanwhile, in a small bowl, stir together soup, sour cream and seasonings. To assemble, slice 2 potatoes into a greased 13"x9" baking pan. Slice 2 eggs; layer on top of potatoes. Gently spread 1/3 of soup mixture on top. Repeat layers 2 more times. Combine bread crumbs and butter in a small bowl; sprinkle over top. Bake, uncovered, at 350 degrees for 30 minutes, or until bubbly and golden. Makes 10 to 12 servings.

No matter where I serve my guests,
They seem to like my kitchen best.
– Old Saying

Grandma's Favorites

Momma's Scalloped Potatoes
Marlys Shomber-Jones
Parsons, KS

This recipe is a little different from the traditional cream sauce potatoes. It is great the next day too, so I always make a big batch. Mom always served it with her special meatloaf, baking the potatoes alongside the meatloaf. These will take awhile to bake, but they are well worth the wait!

10-3/4 oz. can cream of
   mushroom soup
1-1/4 c. milk
3 c. shredded Cheddar cheese,
   divided

4 to 5 potatoes, peeled, very
   thinly sliced and divided
1 onion, very thinly sliced
   and divided
salt and pepper to taste

Whisk together soup and milk in a bowl; set aside. Reserve one cup cheese for topping. Spray a 3-quart casserole dish with non-stick vegetable spray. Layer 1/4 each of potatoes and onion; season with salt and pepper. Add 1/4 of remaining cheese and 1/4 of soup mixture. Repeat layering, making 4 layers. Top with reserved cheese. Bake at 400 degrees for 1-1/2 to 2 hours; cover with aluminum foil if potatoes begin to brown too fast. Makes 6 to 8 servings.

Hosting a big family get-together? Just before everyone digs in, take a snapshot of Grandma's special rolls or the casserole that everyone always begs Aunt Betty to bring! Frame it with the actual recipe for a family memento.

Fresh-Picked from
Grandma's Garden

Cabbage & Fettuccine with Bacon

Ginny Watson
Scranton, PA

*When I was growing up, Gram often made this dish to serve
with pan-fried sausages from a local butcher shop.*

16-oz. pkg. fettuccine pasta,
   uncooked
1/2 lb. bacon, diced
3/4 c. onion, chopped

1 head cabbage, finely chopped
1/2 t. paprika
1 t. salt
1/8 t. pepper

Cook pasta according to package directions; drain. Meanwhile, in a large
skillet over medium heat, cook bacon until crisp. Drain and return bacon
to skillet; reserve 1/4 cup drippings in skillet. Add remaining ingredients
to skillet. Cover and cook for 20 minutes; stirring occasionally. Toss
cabbage mixture with cooked pasta. Makes 6 to 8 servings.

Auntie B's Potato Puffs

Bethi Hendrickson
Danville, PA

*I will forever think of my Auntie B when I make these delicious
crispy little potato balls. They take me back to our family
dinners in the 1970s.*

1 c. mashed potatoes
1 egg, beaten
1/2 c. all-purpose flour
1 t. baking powder

2 T. milk
2 c. canola oil
Garnish: favorite condiments

In a bowl, combine potatoes, egg, flour, baking powder and milk; mix
well. Heat oil in a shallow saucepan over medium-high heat. Drop
potato mixture into hot oil by teaspoonfuls; cook until golden and puffed
up. Cool on a paper towel-lined plate. Serve warm, garnished as desired.
Serves 6 to 8.

Mom's Baked Beans

Pat Rodgers
Katy, TX

This is some good eating! Mom used to make this for every picnic, family reunion, celebration and special meal. She always used a ceramic bean pot with a vented lid. I still have that bean pot and think of her every time I make these beans.

15-oz. can pork & beans	1 c. white onion, chopped
15-oz. can chili beans	1/2 c. barbecue sauce
15-oz. can black beans	1/2 c. brown sugar, packed
15-oz. can kidney beans	2 T. molasses
1 lb. thick-sliced bacon, diced	1/3 c. catsup

Set a colander over a large bowl or pan. Add all beans to colander and allow to drain; reserve bean juice. Transfer beans to a lightly greased 3-quart bean pot or casserole dish; set aside. Meanwhile, in a large skillet over medium heat, cook bacon until crisp; remove bacon to a paper towel-lined plate. Add onion to drippings in skillet; cook until translucent. Return bacon to mixture in skillet; stir well and pour over beans. Stir in remaining ingredients. If mixture seems too thick, add some of the reserved bean juice. Add lid for juicy beans; leave uncovered if a dryer consistency is preferred. Bake at 325 degrees for 2 hours. Let stand 10 minutes before serving. Makes 12 servings.

Dried beans are inexpensive, flavorful and come in lots of varieties. In a recipe, for each 15-ounce can of beans you'll need about 3/4 cup of the dried beans. Soak overnight, drain and prepare as you like.

Pop's Skillet Corn

Marcia Shaffer
Conneaut Lake, PA

Pop loved this dish because it used all the corn off the cob he had had worked hard to grow. He would ask Mother for her angel food cake pan and he would set it on the table, on top of a few paper bags or newspapers. After cutting off the kernels, he would scrape the cobs to get all the juices, which we called corn white milk. We loved his skillet corn...it is so good!

3 to 4 ears sweet corn, kernels
   cut off and cobs reserved
1/4 c. butter, sliced
1/2 c. water
2 T. sugar

1/2 t. salt
1/4 t. pepper
1/4 c. milk
1 T. all-purpose flour

Scrape corn cobs with a knife, reserving the juices. In a 10" cast-iron skillet, combine corn, juices, butter, water, sugar and seasonings. Cover and simmer over medium heat for 15 minutes, stirring occasionally. In a small bowl, combine milk with flour; blend until smooth and stir into corn. Cook for another 5 minutes, stirring often, until thickened. Makes 4 servings.

When cutting the kernels from ears of sweet corn, stand the ear in the center of an angel food cake pan. The kernels will fall neatly into the pan.

Dilly Beans

Marsha Houston
Crossville, TN

My sons loved these crisp, crunchy beans as much as dill pickles!
Works best with very young slender green beans.

4 heads fresh dill weed	4 cloves garlic, peeled
4 1-pint canning jars and lids, sterilized	1 t. cayenne pepper
	2-1/2 c. water
2 lbs. slender green beans, ends trimmed	2-1/2 c. vinegar
	1/4 c. pickling salt

Place one head dill weed in each hot sterilized jar. Pack beans upright into jars, leaving 1/4-inch headspace. To each jar, add one clove garlic and 1/4 teaspoon cayenne pepper; set aside. Combine water, vinegar and pickling salt in a saucepan over medium heat; bring to a boil. Ladle hot mixture into jars, leaving 1/4-inch headspace. Wipe rims; secure with lids and rings. Process in a boiling-water bath for 10 minutes. Set jars on a towel to cool. Check for seals. Makes 4 pints.

Pickling or canning salt, used in many canning recipes, is formulated to dissolve quickly and won't turn the brine cloudy. Look for it next to regular table salt.

Fresh-Picked from
Grandma's Garden

Grandma Lange's Corn Relish

Tammy Ahrens
Sparta, MI

Our neighbors Mr. & Mrs. Lange lived across the field from our house. Though we weren't actually related, we called them "Grandma & Grandpa Lange." We were separated by their amazing garden, which provided many of the ingredients for this delicious recipe. Grandma Lange would open a jar of corn relish for a special treat whenever we gathered around her country table!

2 c. tomatoes, chopped
1 cucumber, peeled and chopped
1 onion, chopped
1 green pepper, chopped
1 c. white vinegar
1 c. sugar

1 T. salt
1-1/2 t. turmeric
1 t. celery seed
4 c. fresh or frozen corn
4 1-pint canning jars and lids,
    sterilized

In a large saucepan, combine all ingredients except corn. Cook over low heat for 40 minutes. Stir in corn. Increase heat to medium and cook 10 minutes more, or until mixture comes to a boil. Ladle hot corn mixture into hot sterilized jars, leaving 1/4-inch headspace. Wipe rims; secure with lids and rings. Process in a boiling-water bath for 15 minutes. Set jars on a towel to cool. Check for seals. Makes 4 pints.

If you're husking heaps of sweet corn, here's an easy tip! Pull on a pair of rubber gloves, then give each cob a quick twist between gloved hands. The corn silk will rub right off.

Mom's Chow Chow

Paula Marchesi
Auburn, PA

Growing up on Long Island, New York, being surrounded with farms, I learned at a young age to use home-grown produce in many interesting ways. I married a farmer and raised two boys on good wholesome farm food. When you live on a farm, you realize nothing should go to waste and nothing beats the taste of fresh. This homemade relish is delicious with all kinds of meat and even seafood. Great on crackers or used as a dip in sour cream too!

7 c. cabbage, shredded
4 c. fresh or frozen corn
4 c. cauliflower, cut into
    small flowerets
2 c. red pepper, diced
1 c. green pepper, diced
1 c. onion, chopped
1/4 c. canning salt
7 c. water, divided

3-1/2 c. brown sugar, packed
1/2 c. all-purpose flour
1/4 c. dry mustard
1 T. celery seed
2 t. turmeric
1-1/2 t. table salt
5 c. cider vinegar
7 1-pint canning jars and lids,
    sterilized

Combine all vegetables in a large bowl; sprinkle with canning salt. Add 6 cups water; cover and refrigerate for 4 hours. Drain and rinse well. In a large heavy saucepan or Dutch oven, combine brown sugar, flour, mustard, celery seed, turmeric and table salt. Stir in vinegar and remaining water until smooth. Bring to a boil; cook and stir for 5 minutes, or until thickened. Add vegetables; bring to a boil. Simmer, uncovered, for 8 to 10 minutes, until crisp-tender. Ladle hot mixture into hot sterilized jars, leaving 1/4-inch headspace. Wipe rims; secure with lids and rings. Process in a boiling-water bath for 15 minutes. Set jars on a towel to cool. Check for seals. Makes 7 pints.

For a boiling-water bath, place canning jars in the kettle about one inch apart, not touching. Add enough water to cover the jars by one to 2 inches.

Fresh-Picked from
Grandma's Garden

Ruth's Pickle Relish

Becky Kuchenbecker
Ravenna, OH

My mother always made this relish when we were growing up. It was a good way to clean out the garden at the end of the season. We add this to deviled eggs, macaroni salad, tuna salad and egg salad, plus many more things. People always comment on how good the food tastes! At my garden club's annual auction, I always take a couple jars of this relish...it always sells!

4 c. onions, coarsely chopped
4 c. cabbage, coarsely chopped
4 c. green tomatoes, coarsely
   chopped
5 c. green peppers, coarsely
   chopped
1-1/2 c. red peppers, coarsely
   chopped
1/2 c. canning salt

6 c. sugar
2 T. mustard seed
1 T. celery seed
1-1/2 t. turmeric
4 c. cider vinegar
2 c. water
9 1-pint canning jars and lids,
   sterilized

Using a food processor, coarsely grind all the vegetables. Combine in a large plastic container and sprinkle with salt; cover and refrigerate overnight. Add vegetables to a colander; rinse and drain. Combine remaining ingredients in a large saucepan; add vegetables. Bring to a boil over high heat; reduce heat to low. Simmer gently until vegetables are almost translucent, about 10 to 15 minutes. Ladle hot mixture into hot sterilized jars, leaving 1/4-inch headspace. Wipe rims; secure with lids and rings. Process in a boiling-water bath for 5 minutes. Set jars on a towel to cool. Check for seals. Makes 9 pints.

Tag sales and flea markets are terrific places to find canning jars. Check for cracks and buy new lids for them. Save old-fashioned jars with one-piece zinc lids to use as vases, tumblers or kitchen canisters.

Yellow Squash Pickles

Karen Hood
Somerset, KY

I have been making these pickles for several years. They were my dad's favorite pickles...he could eat a jar in two days! They are crunchy with such a good flavor. Make extra, because anyone who tries them will want a jar.

8 c. yellow squash, sliced
2 c. onions, sliced
3 green peppers, sliced
1/2 c. pickling salt
3 c. sugar
1 t. mustard seed

1 t. celery seed
1 t. turmeric
2 c. cider vinegar
1 T. all-purpose flour
8 to 10 1-pint canning jars
   and lids, sterilized

Combine squash, onions and peppers in a large non-metallic bowl; cover with ice water and salt. Let stand for 2 hours. Drain; rinse with cold water and set aside. In a large kettle, combine sugar and spices. Combine vinegar and flour in a small bowl; mix well and add to kettle. Stir well; bring to a boil over medium heat. Add squash mixture; return just to a boil and remove from heat. Ladle hot mixture into hot sterilized jars, leaving 1/4-inch headspace. Wipe rims; secure with lids and rings. Process in a boiling-water bath for 10 minutes. Set jars on a towel to cool. Check for seals. Makes 8 to 10 pints.

To sterilize canning jars and lids, submerge them in water, bring to a boil, reduce heat and allow to simmer for 10 minutes. Remove from heat, but leave jars and lids in the hot water until ready to fill and use.

Fresh-Picked from
Grandma's Garden

Fresh-From-the-Garden Crunchy Pickles

Sheila Peregrin
Lancaster, PA

This is a great recipe because it is so fast to make and is sooooo delicious! I make these pickles all year long...they are just as good on an Easter relish tray or tucked into a Christmas gift basket for a friend as they are at a summer cookout! The onion slices are simply wonderful on a meatloaf sandwich.

1 large cucumber, sliced 1/4-inch thick
1 onion, thinly sliced and separated into rings
1 c. sugar

1/2 c. white or cider vinegar
1/2 t. mustard seed
1/4 t. celery seed
1/4 t. turmeric
1/2 t. salt

Combine all ingredients in a large microwave-safe bowl. Microwave on high for about 7 to 8 minutes, stirring every 3 minutes, until onion is translucent. Transfer to a glass or plastic storage container; cover and refrigerate. For best flavor, allow the flavors to blend for a day before serving. Makes about 2-1/2 cups.

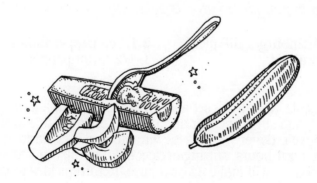

Seed a cucumber in seconds! Cut it in half lengthwise and run a spoon down the center, scooping out the seeds.

Grandma's Favorites

Candied Dill Pickles

Barbara Imler
Noblesville, IN

I'm a pickle lover, and I especially enjoy these candied dills because you can taste both sweet and dill pickles in every bite!

32-oz. jar dill pickle spears
   without garlic, drained
1/2 c. tarragon vinegar

2-3/4 c. sugar
2 T. mixed pickling spices

Rinse out pickle jar and lid; set aside. Combine vinegar and sugar in a large glass or plastic bowl; stir in pickles. Tie pickling spices in a piece of cheesecloth; add to bowl and stir. Cover and let stand at room temperature for 4 to 5 hours, until sugar dissolves, stirring occasionally. Add half of the pickles to the empty jar; add spice bag and remaining pickles. Add vinegar mixture; cover and refrigerate at least 4 days before serving. Discard spice bag after one week. Will keep a long time in the refrigerator. Makes one quart.

Fire & Ice Pickles

Nan Scarborough
Farmerville, LA

These are the best and easiest pickles! Serve them as a side, or pack them in pint jars to give as gifts. Anyone can make these.

32-oz. jar hamburger dill pickle
   chips, drained
2 c. sugar

2 T. red pepper flakes
1-1/2 t. hot pepper sauce

Rinse out pickle jar and lid; set aside. Place pickles in a large glass or plastic bowl; add sugar, pepper and hot sauce. Stir with a wooden spoon until mixed well. Cover with plastic wrap to seal. Let stand at room temperature for 4 hours, stirring occasionally to mix and covering after each stir. Mixture will make its own juice. Return pickles to jar; add lid and refrigerate. Pickles are ready to serve immediately; flavor is best after refrigerated overnight. Keep refrigerated. Makes one quart.

Fresh-Picked from
Grandma's Garden

Grandma Bradley's Zucchini Jam
Vanessa Fleming
Du Quoin, IL

My grandmother always made several different jams and jellies during the growing seasons. This one was a favorite of mine. I was delighted when we found the recipe tucked away among some of her favorite recipes.

2 oranges, divided
5 c. zucchini, peeled and ends
    trimmed
5 c. sugar
3 T. lemon juice

6-oz. can frozen orange juice
    concentrate, thawed
6-oz. pkg. orange gelatin mix
5 to 6 1-pint canning jars and
    lids, sterilized

Coarsely cut up one orange with peel still on; grind in a food mill and transfer to a bowl. Peel remaining orange, discarding peel. Grind orange sections; add to bowl and set aside. Grind zucchini; combine zucchini and sugar in a large saucepan. Add ground oranges, lemon juice and orange juice. Bring to a low boil over medium heat. Simmer for 12 minutes, stirring often. Add gelatin; cook and stir until gelatin is dissolved. Ladle hot mixture into hot sterilized jars, leaving 1/4-inch headspace. Wipe rims; secure with lids and rings. Keep refrigerated. Makes 5 to 6 pints.

Bottle up homemade pickles or preserves in glass jelly jars for gift giving and add a calico topper...sure to be appreciated!

Spicy Apple Pie Jam

Jennifer Parr
Ontario, Canada

If you like apple pie with a sprinkle of cinnamon, you will love this jam. It's very rich and so delicious. All my friends make it too.

2 c. Granny Smith apples, peeled, cored and finely chopped
1/3 c. golden raisins
1 c. water
1/3 c. lemon juice
1-1/2 t. cinnamon
1/2 t. allspice

4-1/2 c. sugar
1 c. brown sugar, packed
1 t. butter
1 pouch liquid pectin
5 1-pint canning jars and lids, sterilized

In a large saucepan, combine apples, raisins, water, lemon juice and spices; stir well. Add sugars; stir to combine. Over high heat, bring mixture to a rolling boil; add butter. Cook and stir until mixture comes to a full boil. Boil hard for one minute; remove from heat and stir in pectin. Stir for 5 minutes; skimming off any foam. Ladle hot mixture into hot sterilized jars, leaving 1/4-inch headspace. Wipe rims; secure with lids and rings. Process in a boiling-water bath for 5 minutes. Set jars on a towel to cool. Check for seals. Makes 5 pints.

Get ready for spur-of-the-moment picnics on sunny days...tuck a basket filled with picnic supplies into the car trunk along with a quilt to sit on. One stop at a roadside farmstand for food and you'll be dining in style!

Fresh-Picked from
Grandma's Garden

Blueberry-Lemon Jam

Bethi Hendrickson
Danville, PA

Fresh berries and lemon make the summer so much better! This jam has two of my favorites and a little extra or two to kick it up a notch. It's always a wonderful treat on those cold winter mornings.

8 c. fresh blueberries
3/4 c. powdered fruit pectin
3 T. lemon juice
1 T. lemon zest
2 t. cinnamon

1/2 t. nutmeg
1 T. butter
6 c. sugar
8 1/2-pint canning jars and
    lids, sterilized

Working in batches, process blueberries in a food processor; transfer to a stockpot. Stir in pectin, lemon juice and zest, spices and butter; mix well. Bring to a boil over medium-high heat. Add sugar; cook and stir until well blended. Over high heat, bring mixture to a rolling boil. Cook, stirring constantly, for one minute. Turn off heat; skim off any foam. Ladle hot mixture into hot sterilized jars, leaving 1/4-inch headspace. Wipe rims; secure with lids and rings. Process in a boiling-water bath for 10 minutes. Set jars on a towel to cool. Check for seals. Let stand for 24 hours before using. Makes 8, 1/2-pint jars.

Host a canning party with friends! Whether you stir up one big kettle of preserves together or make several flavors of easy freezer jams, you'll all have sweet souvenirs to take home. Be sure to have lots of vanilla wafers and cream cheese for sampling!

Grandma's Favorites

Cranberry-Apple Relish

Joyceann Dreibelbis
Wooster, OH

When winter comes, these jewel-toned jars of summer bounty will taste better than ever! And who wouldn't want a jar of homemade relish as a gift?

1 lb. tart apples, peeled, cored
   and chopped
4 c. fresh cranberries, coarsely
   chopped
2-1/2 c. brown sugar, packed

1 c. water
1/2 c. chopped walnuts
1/2 t. cinnamon
5 1/2-pint canning jars and
   lids, sterilized

Combine apples, cranberries, brown sugar and water in a large saucepan. Simmer over medium heat for 15 minutes, stirring frequently. Stir in walnuts and cinnamon; continue cooking for 5 minutes. Ladle hot mixture into hot sterilized jars, leaving 1/4-inch headspace. Wipe rims; secure with lids and rings. Process in a boiling-water bath for 15 minutes. Set jars on a towel to cool. Check for seals. Makes about 5, 1/2-pint jars.

Candy Apple Jelly

Lee Beedle
Church View, VA

I made this recipe while my parents and niece and nephew were visiting with us. My niece liked it so much, she asked me to make a batch for her to take home! That took me back in time 35 years or more, to when my aunt would do the same for me.

4 c. apple juice or cider
1/2 c. red cinnamon candies
1-3/4 oz. pkg. powdered fruit
   pectin

4-1/2 c. sugar
6 1/2-pt. canning jars and
   lids, sterilized

Combine juice or cider, candies and pectin in a large heavy saucepan. Bring to a full boil over high heat, stirring constantly. Stir in sugar; return to a full boil. Boil for 2 minutes, stirring constantly. Remove from heat. Skim off foam and any unmelted candies. Ladle hot mixture into hot sterilized jars, leaving 1/4-inch headspace. Wipe rims; secure with lids and rings. Process in a boiling-water bath for 5 minutes. Set jars on a towel to cool. Check for seals. Makes 6, 1/2-pint jars.

Fresh-Picked from
Grandma's Garden

Grandmother's Pear Honey

Paula Mihm
Baltimore, MD

My grandmother would always make this, but never had a written recipe. It gets its name from being thick and honey-colored. I worked hard to find out how to do it, and after several tries, my daddy said that it was even better then hers. Scrumptious on homemade hot biscuits or bread!

16 c. Bartlett or Bosc pears,
    peeled, cored and chopped
20-oz. can crushed pineapple in
    syrup

10 c. sugar
1 T. lemon juice
12 to 16 1/2-pint canning jars
    and lids, sterilized

Combine chopped pears, pineapple with syrup, sugar and lemon juice in a stockpot. Bring to a boil over medium-high heat; reduce heat to medium. Cook, stirring occasionally, until pears are tender and mixture thickens, about 30 minutes. Ladle hot mixture into hot sterilized jars, leaving 1/4-inch headspace. Wipe rims; secure with lids and rings. Process in a boiling-water bath for 10 minutes. Set jars on a towel to cool. Check for seals. Makes 12 to 16, 1/2-pint jars.

Make a cut-glass relish tray sparkle like diamonds. Wash it in mild dish soap, then rinse well with a mixture that's half plain warm water and half white vinegar. Pat dry with a lint-free towel.

Grandma's Favorites

Peachy Pepper Preserves

April Garner
Independence, KY

This is great as a glaze for ham or pork roast, or spooned over a block of cream cheese to serve as an appetizer.

4-1/2 c. peaches, peeled, pitted
   and diced
1-1/2 c. sugar
3 T. lime juice
1 T. jalapeño pepper, finely
   chopped

1/2 roasted red pepper, finely
   chopped
1-3/4 oz. pkg. powdered fruit
   pectin
6 to 8 1-pint canning jars and
   lids, sterilized

Combine all ingredients in a microwave-safe container. Microwave on high for 8 minutes; mixture will boil. Stir; microwave on high another 8 to 10 minutes, until thickened to the consistency of pancake syrup. Ladle into hot sterilized jars; wipe rims, add lids and cool completely, about 2 hours. Cover and store in refrigerator up to 3 weeks. Makes 6 to 8 pints.

Easy Peach Marmalade

LuLu Combs
Aberdeen, MD

This recipe has great homemade flavor without a lot of fuss. The color of your preserves depends on the flavor of gelatin you choose. Makes a wonderful gift!

5 c. peaches, peeled, pitted
   and mashed
7 c. sugar
2 c. canned crushed pineapple,
   well drained

6-oz. pkg. peach, apricot, orange
   or raspberry gelatin mix
5 1-pint canning jars or freezer
   containers and lids, sterilized

Combine peaches, sugar and pineapple in a stockpot over high heat. Bring to a boil; reduce heat to medium-high and boil for 15 minutes. Add gelatin; stir until dissolved. Ladle into hot sterilized jars or containers; wipe rims, add lids and refrigerate. If using freezer containers, allow to cool; add lids and freeze. Makes 5 pints.

Grandma's Best
Supper Dishes

Chicken & Spinach Cambrini

Lauren Steinbauer
Columbus, OH

This recipe is from my grandma. I remember her always being in the kitchen, making dinners and pies for the whole family. Whenever I make this recipe, I smile and think of her.

16-oz. pkg. spaghetti, uncooked
2 boneless, skinless chicken
  breasts, cooked and diced
2 10-oz. pkgs. frozen spinach,
  cooked and drained
16-oz. container sour cream
8-oz. can sliced mushrooms,
  drained

1/4 c. onion, chopped
1/2 c. butter, melted
8-oz. pkg. shredded Monterey
  Jack cheese
8-oz. pkg. shredded mozzarella
  cheese
salt and pepper to taste

Cook spaghetti according to package directions; drain. Meanwhile, combine remaining ingredients in a large bowl. Add cooked spaghetti; toss to mix well. Spread mixture in a greased deep 13"x9" baking pan. Cover and bake at 375 degrees for 15 minutes. Uncover; bake another 15 minutes, or until bubbly and cheese is melted. Makes 10 servings.

Make a double batch of your favorite comfort food and invite the neighbors over for supper...what a great way to get to know them better. Keep it simple with a tossed salad, warm bakery bread and apple crisp for dessert. It's all about food and fellowship!

Supper Dishes

One-Pan Cabbage Roll Casserole

Kristine Pennington
Lakewood, CO

Whenever I make this casserole, I think of my German grandmother and her hearty cabbage rolls! Sauerkraut takes the place of cabbage and saves a lot of chopping.

2 lbs. ground beef
1 c. onion, chopped
2 cloves garlic, minced
1 T. olive oil
28-oz. can crushed tomatoes
8-oz. can tomato sauce

28-oz. can sauerkraut, drained
1 c. long-cooking rice, uncooked
1 t. salt
1/2 t. pepper
2 14-oz. cans beef broth

In a large skillet over medium-high heat, cook beef, onion and garlic in olive oil until beef is no longer pink. Drain; set aside. Meanwhile, in a large bowl, combine tomatoes with juice, tomato sauce, sauerkraut, rice and seasonings. Add beef mixture; mix well. Transfer mixture to a greased deep 13"x9" baking pan. Pour broth over beef mixture. Bake, covered, at 350 degrees for one hour; stir. Cover again and bake for another 30 minutes. Serves 8.

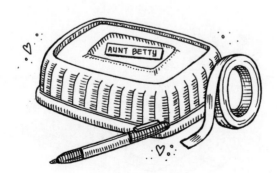

Help a potluck hostess keep track of all the casserole dishes.
Jot down your name on a piece of tape with a permanent marker
and attach it to the bottom of the baking pan.

Easy Cheesy Beefy Mac

Heather McDowell
Oak Hill, WV

I used to love to come home from school on cold, snowy days. Mom would have a hearty dish like this one simmering on the stove and a simple tossed salad chilling in the fridge. It's still nice to serve this dish to the family sitting around the dinner table, sharing stories from years ago. Be sure to include everyone with their own unique story!

12-oz. pkg. elbow macaroni,
    uncooked
1-1/2 lbs. ground beef sirloin
1 c. onion, chopped
2 t. garlic powder
1 T. dried parsley
Optional: 1/2 t. salt, 1 t. pepper

2 14-1/2 oz. cans petite diced
    tomatoes
8-oz. pkg. pasteurized process
    cheese spread, cubed
10-oz. pkg. frozen corn
Garnish: dried parsley

Cook macaroni according to package directions; drain. Meanwhile, in a large skillet over medium heat, brown beef with onion; drain and add seasonings. Stir in tomatoes with juice and cheese; reduce heat to very low and stir until cheese melts. Stir in cooked macaroni. Continue simmering over very low heat until well blended; do not overcook macaroni. Add corn; cook over low heat until tender. Garnish with parsley. Serves 6 to 8.

When chopping onions, celery or green peppers, it takes only
a moment to chop some extras. Tuck them away in the fridge
or freezer for a quick start to dinner another day.

Spaghetti di Contadino

Sharon Velenosi
Costa Mesa, CA

My Nonni always cooked with her own homemade ingredients. She would make her own prosciutto and kept it hanging in the cellar. Whenever she needed some, she would go down to the cellar and cut off a piece. So many wonderful things were in that cellar, nothing from a store...everything from the garden and homemade. This simple peasant-style recipe is so easy and oh-so Italian.

12-oz. pkg. spaghetti, uncooked
1 lb. tomatoes, chopped
1 T. garlic, minced
1 T. olive oil
5-oz. pkg. prosciutto, minced

1/2 t. pepper
1/4 t. dried oregano
Garnish: chopped fresh parsley,
   grated Parmesan cheese

Cook spaghetti according to package directions; drain. Meanwhile, in a skillet over medium heat, sauté tomatoes and garlic in oil until tender, about 5 minutes. Add prosciutto and seasonings. Reduce heat to low; simmer until ingredients are blended, about 2 to 3 minutes. Toss tomato mixture with cooked spaghetti. Sprinkle with parsley and serve with Parmesan cheese. Makes 4 servings.

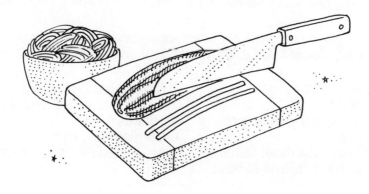

Lighten up a pasta recipe...make "zoodles" from zucchini or summer squash. Use a spiralizer or a sharp knife to cut squash into long, thin strips. Steam lightly or sauté in a little olive oil and toss with your favorite pasta sauce.

Grandmama King's Mustard Gravy Chicken

Jill Luffman
Mount Juliet, TN

My grandmama made this recipe for us back in the 1970s.
My mom has continued to make it and now, so do I.
We love it...so good with navy beans, turnips and cornbread!

4 chicken breasts	2-1/2 T. mustard
2-1/2 T. all-purpose flour	1 T. sugar
salt and pepper to taste	3 T. vinegar

Cover chicken with water in a saucepan. Cook over medium heat until chicken juices run clear, 25 to 35 minutes. Remove chicken to a bowl, reserving broth. Cool; shred chicken, discarding skin and bones. Place chicken in a greased 13"x9" baking pan; set aside. Add remaining ingredients to reserved broth; stir into a paste. Cook over low heat until thickened, adding a little water if too thick. Spoon mixture over chicken in pan. Bake, uncovered, at 350 degrees for 15 minutes, or until hot and bubbly. Serves 4.

Creamy Tomato-Basil Pasta

Brandi Talton
Guyton, GA

This is my go-to recipe when I want some good ol' comfort food. Serve with a salad and garlic bread for a great Italian meal!

12-oz. pkg. bowtie pasta, uncooked	2 T. fresh basil, chopped
1 lb. sweet Italian ground pork sausage	Optional: 1/2 to 1 T. red pepper flakes
2 14-1/2 oz. cans diced tomatoes with garlic, oregano & basil	1 c. whipping cream
	1/2 c. grated Parmesan cheese

Cook pasta according to package directions; drain. Meanwhile, brown sausage in a skillet over medium heat; drain and return to pan. Stir in tomatoes with juice, basil and red pepper flakes, if using. Cook for 10 minutes, or until a sauce forms. Stir in cream and Parmesan cheese; simmer for about 15 more minutes, but do not boil. Serve sauce ladled over cooked pasta. Makes 6 servings.

Chicken's Nest

Cherie Clark
North Hyde Park, VT

I use to make this recipe with my grandmother, and I still make it today. It can also be made with biscuits instead of stuffing. This dish can be made ahead of time, then frozen baked or unbaked.

3-lb. deli rotisserie chicken
6-oz. pkg. chicken-flavored
  stuffing mix
16-oz. container sour cream
8-oz. pkg. cream cheese,
  softened

10-3/4 oz. can cream of chicken
  soup
16-oz. pkg. frozen chopped
  broccoli, cooked
Optional: 1/2 c. sugar or
  1/4 c. sweetener

Slice chicken or cut into serving-size pieces. Arrange chicken in a greased 13"x9" baking pan; set aside. Prepare stuffing mix according to package directions; set aside. In a bowl, blend together sour cream, cream cheese and soup; fold in broccoli and sugar or sweetener, if using. To assemble, spread half of sour cream mixture over chicken; add half of stuffing. Repeat layers. Cover and bake at 350 degrees for 20 minutes. Uncover; bake 10 more minutes, or until hot and bubbly. Makes 8 servings.

Share funny memories at the next family get-together. Ask everyone to jot down their favorites and toss them in a hat. Pull them out one at a time to read out loud...guaranteed giggles!

Grandma's Favorites

Baked Pork Chops & Apples

Beth Flack
Terre Haute, IN

This recipe is a family favorite that my grandmother used to make in the fall. Perfect after you've gone apple picking!

2 T. margarine
6 pork chops
1/2 c. onion, chopped
1/2 t. dried rosemary
3/4 t. salt

1/8 t. pepper
3/4 c. water
3 red apples, cored and sliced
   crosswise

Melt margarine in a large skillet over medium-high heat. Add pork chops; cook until browned on both sides. Remove pork chops to a greased 13"x9" baking pan; set aside. Add onion and seasonings to drippings in skillet; reduce heat to medium and cook for 5 minutes. Stir in water. Arrange apple slices over pork chops; spoon onion mixture over top. Cover with aluminum foil. Bake at 350 degrees for one hour. Makes 6 servings.

Ruth's Lazy Man Pierogi

Tammy Pickering
Fairport, NY

My mother made this often when I was a child because she knew how much I loved it. She even made it for my high school graduation party. Now my daughter can enjoy it too!

16-oz. pkg. rotini pasta,
   uncooked
1-lb. Polish pork sausage link,
   skin removed and crumbled
10-3/4 oz. can cream of
   mushroom soup

14-oz. can sauerkraut, drained
   and rinsed
8-oz. can sliced mushrooms,
   drained

Cook pasta according to package directions, just until tender; drain. Meanwhile, brown sausage in a skillet over medium heat; transfer to a lightly greased 2-quart casserole dish. Add cooked pasta and remaining ingredients; mix gently. Bake, uncovered, at 350 degrees for 25 minutes, or until bubbly. Makes 4 to 6 servings.

Supper Dishes

Hungarian Sauerkraut & Pork

Patricia Owens
Middle Bass, OH

This recipe is from my grandmother, who emigrated to the United States in 1906. It's a family favorite and one of my favorite comfort foods. I save time by using pork cubes that are sold pre-packaged for making city chicken.

2 T. shortening
2 lbs. boneless lean pork, cubed
1 T. Hungarian paprika
1 t. salt

32-oz. pkg. refrigerated
   sauerkraut, drained
1/2 c. water
8-oz. container sour cream

Melt shortening in a large skillet over medium heat. Add pork cubes and brown on all sides; drain. Season pork cubes with paprika and salt; return to skillet. Rinse sauerkraut, if desired; add to skillet along with water. Cover and simmer over low heat for one hour, adding more water as needed. Gradually blend in sour cream; simmer over low heat, until heated through. Makes 4 to 5 servings.

Stir some seasoned salt and coarsely ground pepper into flour,
then fill a big shaker to keep by the side of the stove.
So handy to sprinkle on meat for pan-frying!

Grandma's Saucy Citrus Fish Dish
Janis Parr
Ontario, Canada

My Grandma Starr was born and raised in England before coming to Canada. She loved all kinds of fish and seafood. While we kids didn't care much for her scallops or periwinkles, we did love this dish, and she would make it for us whenever we visited her.

2 lbs. haddock, halibut or	1 t. orange zest
cod fillets	1 t. dried parsley
1/4 c. butter	1 t. salt
2 c. mushrooms, chopped	1/4 t. pepper
1/4 c. green onions, chopped	2 T. all-purpose flour
1 t. lemon zest	1 c. cold milk

Arrange fish fillets in a greased 13"x9" baking pan; set aside. Melt butter in a skillet over medium heat; sauté mushrooms and onions. Stir in citrus zests and seasonings. In a small bowl, stir flour into cold milk. Slowly stir milk mixture into mushroom mixture in skillet until sauce is thickened; spoon sauce over fish. Bake, uncovered, at 350 degrees for 30 minutes, or until fish flakes easily. Makes 4 servings.

Encourage children to take a no-thank-you helping, or just one bite, of foods they think they don't like...they may be pleasantly surprised!

Supper Dishes

Shrimp & Everything

Judy Henfey
Cibolo, TX

*My mom made this recipe often as I was growing up. It is now
in my recipe box and is a quick weeknight dinner. Serve with
a fresh green salad and crunchy French bread.*

1 T. oil
1 lb. uncooked medium shrimp,
  peeled and cleaned
1/2 c. onion, chopped
1/2 c. green pepper, cut into
  thin strips
1/2 c. celery, thinly sliced

14-1/2 oz. can stewed tomatoes
8-oz. can tomato sauce
1 t. hot pepper sauce, or to taste
1/2 t. dried thyme
1/2 t. garlic powder
1-1/2 c. instant rice, uncooked
Optional: chopped fresh parsley

Heat oil in a large skillet over medium heat. Add shrimp, onions, pepper
strips and celery. Cook and stir until shrimp are pink. Add tomatoes
with juice, tomato sauce, hot sauce, thyme and garlic powder; bring to
a boil. Stir in rice; cover and remove from heat. Let stand for 5 to
6 minutes; fluff with a fork. Sprinkle with parsley, if desired. Makes
4 servings.

Turn leftover hot dog buns into slices of garlic bread in a jiffy...
easy for little hands to help make. Spread with softened butter,
sprinkle with garlic salt and broil until toasty and golden.

Chicken Fricassee

Shirley Howie
Foxboro, MA

This dish brings back pleasant memories of my childhood, as Mom made it often! I have updated the recipe a bit with a shorter cooking time, using chicken breasts, but you could use any chicken pieces that you prefer.

1/4 c. all-purpose flour
1 t. salt
1/2 t. pepper
1 t. paprika
4 boneless, skinless chicken
   breasts
2 T. olive oil

1/2 c. onion, sliced
2 to 3 stalks celery, thinly sliced
2 to 3 carrots, thinly sliced
10-3/4 oz. can cream of
   chicken soup
1-1/2 c. milk
cooked rice or egg noodles

Combine flour, salt, pepper and paprika in a plastic zipping bag. Add chicken to bag, one piece at a time; close and shake well to coat. Heat oil in a large skillet over medium-high heat. Add chicken; cook until golden on all sides. Remove chicken from skillet to a plate. Add vegetables to drippings in skillet; cook until tender, stirring occasionally. Return chicken to skillet. In a bowl, whisk together soup and milk; spoon over chicken and stir to combine. Bring to a boil; reduce heat to low. Cover and simmer for 30 minutes, or until chicken is tender. Serve chicken and sauce over cooked rice or noodles. Makes 4 servings.

Steamed rice that's tender...never mushy! Cook rice according to package directions, then remove pan from heat, cover with a folded tea towel and replace the lid. Let stand for 5 to 10 minutes, fluff with a fork and serve. The towel will absorb any excess moisture.

Grandma's Best
Supper Dishes

Neena's Southern Mac & Cheese

Lynne Doughan
Britt, IA

Living in Iowa in the wintertime, there are days when the temperature with the wind chill can be 25 to 40 below. Brrrrr! Being from Mississippi, I really crave my MawMaw's macaroni & cheese. On those cold days, it's so yummy and easy! Served as either a main dish or a side, it's delish.

8-oz. pkg. small shell macaroni,
   uncooked
1/2 c. plus 2 T. butter, divided
1/2 c. cornstarch
1 T. salt
1 T. pepper
4 c. buttermilk or whole milk
6 c. shredded sharp Cheddar
   cheese, divided
1/2 c. panko bread crumbs

Cook macaroni according to package directions; drain. Meanwhile, melt 1/2 cup butter in a large saucepan over medium heat. Add cornstarch; cook and whisk for 2 to 3 minutes. Add salt and pepper. Slowly whisk in buttermilk or milk until thickened. Remove from heat. In a buttered 13"x9" baking pan, layer half of cooked macaroni and half of cheese. Repeat layers; pour milk mixture over top. Let stand for one to 2 minutes, until cheese melts; stir and set aside. In a skillet over low heat, melt remaining butter; add bread crumbs and stir until golden. Sprinkle crumb mixture over casserole. Bake, uncovered, at 350 degrees for 12 to 15 minutes, until bubbly and golden. Makes 8 servings.

Napkin rings are simple to make. Just sew buttons, charms or fabric yo-yo's onto a 6-inch length of elastic. Stitch the ends together and you're done!

Nanny Smith's Angel Hair Pasta Marinara

Marge Smith
Tulsa, OK

My brother-in-law shared this recipe with me many years ago, when I was a new wife learning to cook. It has become a meal our family enjoys a couple times a month.

7-oz. pkg. angel hair pasta, uncooked
2 T. extra-virgin olive oil
14-oz. pkg. skinless smoked beef sausage, chopped
1 onion, coarsely chopped
1 green pepper, coarsely chopped

1 t. garlic, minced
2 15-oz. cans tomato sauce
14-1/2 oz. can petite diced tomatoes
1/3 c. balsamic vinegar
Garnish: 1 c. shaved Parmesan cheese

Cook pasta according to package directions; drain. Meanwhile, add olive oil to a skillet over medium heat; add sausage, onion, pepper and garlic. Cook until sausage is lightly golden and vegetables are crisp-tender; drain. Stir in tomato sauce, tomatoes with juice and vinegar; heat through. To serve, ladle sauce over cooked pasta; garnish with Parmesan cheese. Makes 4 servings.

Boiling a big pot of water for pasta? Cover it with a lid...
it'll come to a boil much more quickly.

Mom's Eggplant Casserole

Michele Menefee
Belmont, OH

This is a recipe that my mother made for us when we were little.
It's been a family favorite for over 50 years.

4 to 5 c. eggplant, peeled
   and cubed
5 to 6 tomatoes, chopped
1 to 2 green peppers, cut into
   chunks
1 c. onion, chopped

1/2 to 3/4 c. instant brown or
   white rice, uncooked
1 c. Cheddar cheese, diced
2 T. bacon drippings or butter
2 T. sugar
salt and pepper to taste

Mix all ingredients together in a large bowl. Transfer mixture into a
16"x12" baking pan sprayed with non-stick vegetable mixture. Cover
with aluminum foil. Bake at 350 degrees for 1-1/2 hours. Uncover and
stir; bake for another 30 minutes. Makes 6 servings.

Make a recipe book of the best handed-down family favorites.
Tie it all up with a bow and slip a family photo in the front...
a gift to be treasured.

Zucchini Italian Pizza Skillet

Maria Kuhns
Crofton, MD

My mother used to make this recipe often in the summertime, when our garden was overflowing with zucchini. It's a twist on pizza, but healthy with veggies! Serve with a crisp side salad and warm, crusty bread.

2 c. elbow macaroni, uncooked
2 T. olive or canola oil
2 to 3 zucchini, peeled and diced
1/2 c. onion, finely diced
1 lb. ground beef
14-1/2 oz. can diced tomatoes
2 8-oz. cans tomato sauce

1/2 t. sugar
1 t. dried oregano
1 t. dried basil
1/2 t. salt
1/2 t. pepper
8-oz. pkg. shredded mozzarella cheese

Cook macaroni according to package directions; drain. Meanwhile, heat oil in a large skillet over medium heat. Add zucchini and onion; sauté until tender. Remove vegetables to a bowl; set aside. Add beef to skillet and cook until no longer pink; drain. Return zucchini and onion to skillet. Stir in tomatoes with juice, tomato sauce, sugar and seasonings. Simmer for 10 minutes, stirring occasionally. Sprinkle with cheese; let stand until melted. Serve over cooked macaroni. Makes 4 servings.

When shopping for cloth napkins, be sure to pick up an extra one! Use it to wrap around a flower pot or vase, and you'll always have a matching centerpiece.

Grandma's Best
Supper Dishes

Hot Dog, Green Pepper & Onion Dinner

Karen Dean
New Market, MD

My Italian grandmother made up this recipe. This dinner was always my father's favorite...he would rather have this than Crab Imperial. It's my favorite too. It's delicious!

1 to 2 T. olive oil
1 clove garlic, minced
6 green peppers, cut into strips
2 onions, sliced
28-oz. can peeled whole
   tomatoes

Italian seasoning, garlic salt,
   salt and pepper to taste
8 beef hot dogs, sliced
1-1/2 c. cooked rice

Add olive oil to cover the bottom of a large saucepan. Add garlic; cook over medium heat until lightly golden. Add peppers and onions; simmer until soft. Add tomatoes with juice; simmer until heated through. Stir in seasonings to taste. Add hot dogs; simmer for another 15 minutes. Serve hot dog mixture spooned over cooked rice. Makes 6 servings.

Storytelling time! After dinner, invite family members to share their most treasured family stories. Be sure to save these special moments by capturing them on video.

121

Oven Sausage & Peppers

Barbara Dell
Bethpage, NY

My mother used to make this yummy recipe for a quick weekend supper. We'd eat it on TV trays while watching football on television.

2 onions, sliced
2 green and/or red peppers, sliced
2 cloves garlic, chopped
1-lb. Italian pork sausage link, cut into chunks
2 T. olive oil

salt and pepper to taste
1/2 c. white wine or chicken broth
buttered egg noodles and grated Parmesan cheese, or garlic hero rolls, split

Toss together onions, peppers and garlic in a greased 13"x9" baking pan. Add sausage; drizzle with olive oil and season with salt and pepper. Drizzle wine or broth over all; cover with aluminum foil. Bake at 375 degrees for 35 minutes. Uncover and bake for 10 minutes more; stir well. Serve sausage mixture over buttered noodles, sprinkled with Parmesan cheese, or spooned into hero rolls. Makes 4 servings.

Stem and seed a bell pepper in a jiffy. Hold the pepper upright on a cutting board. Use a sharp knife to slice each of the sides from the pepper. You'll then have 4 large seedless pieces ready for chopping!

Grandma's Best
Supper Dishes

Shaggy Tigers

Karen Koch
McLouth, KS

*This old recipe for beef patties is from my aunt's collection
from the 1950s. They're still tasty and easy to make.*

1 lb. ground beef
1 egg, beaten
1/2 c. potato, peeled and grated
1/4 c. onion, chopped
1/4 c. milk or tomato juice

1 t. salt
1/4 t. pepper
Garnish: catsup, mustard
    or barbecue sauce

In a large bowl, combine all ingredients except garnish; mix very well.
Shape into 4 to 5 thick oval patties; place in a greased 13"x9" baking
pan. Bake, uncovered, at 425 degrees for 25 minutes, or until no longer
pink in the center. Garnish as desired. Serves 4 to 5.

Momma's Rice Meatballs

Tammy Navarro
Littleton, CO

*My mother used to make these easy and delicious meatballs for us
while we were growing up. She's gone now, but now I make them
for my family and always think of her when I do.*

1 lb. ground beef
1 c. instant rice, uncooked
1 egg, beaten
46-oz. can tomato juice, divided

2 to 3 T. sugar
mashed potatoes or cooked
    egg noodles

In a bowl, combine beef, rice, egg and 1/2 cup tomato juice. Mix well;
roll into one-inch meatballs. Combine remaining tomato juice and sugar
in a large saucepan over medium heat; bring to a full boil. Carefully add
meatballs; cover and reduce heat to medium-low. Continue cooking
until the meatballs are done, about 25 minutes. Serve with mashed
potatoes or spooned over egg noodles. Serves 6.

For tasty sliders, flatten your favorite
meatball mixture into small patties. Bake
as usual and serve on small buns.

Slow-Cooker Cheesy Chicken Tetrazzini

Sydney Smith
Ontario, Canada

This recipe has been a staple for all the women in my family. It was handed down from my grandmother, to my mother, to me. It is absolutely delectable and is sure to wow any crowd!

3 to 4 boneless, skinless chicken breasts, halved
2 onions, chopped
2 cloves garlic, minced
1/4 c. fresh parsley, minced
2 c. water
1 c. white wine or chicken broth
1/2 t. dried thyme
2 t. salt
1/2 t. pepper

2/3 c. butter, sliced
2/3 c. all-purpose flour
1 c. light cream or whole milk
16-oz. pkg. spaghetti, broken into 2-inch pieces and uncooked
1/2 lb. mushrooms, chopped
Garnish: 1 c. grated Parmesan cheese

In a 5-quart slow cooker, combine chicken, onions, garlic, parsley, water, wine or broth and seasonings. Cover and cook on low setting for 8 to 10 hours, or on high setting for 4 to 5 hours, until chicken is well done. Remove chicken and cool; strain broth into a bowl and set aside. Cut chicken into bite-sized pieces and set aside. Add butter to slow cooker; turn to high setting. When butter is melted, stir in flour. Gradually pour in reserved broth and cream or milk. Cook on high setting for 30 minutes. Meanwhile, cook spaghetti according to package directions; drain. Add spaghetti, chicken and mushrooms to slow cooker. Cover and cook for another 15 minutes. Season with additional salt and pepper, as desired. Sprinkle with Parmesan cheese and serve. Makes 4 to 6 servings.

Keep a ball of kitchen string right where you need it! Simply drop it into a small teapot and pull out the end of the string through the spout.

Grandma's Best
Supper Dishes

Slow-Cooker Chicken Stew

Jeanne Koebel
Adirondack, NY

A super-easy and hearty meal. Bake some biscuits to go with it!

2 16-oz. pkgs. frozen stew
   vegetables, thawed
8 to 10 boneless, skinless
   chicken thighs
1/2 t. dried rosemary

1/2 t. onion powder
1/4 t. paprika
2 10-oz. cans chicken gravy
10-oz. pkg. frozen baby peas,
   thawed

Spray a 5-quart slow cooker with non-stick vegetable spray; add thawed
stew vegetables. Place chicken on top; sprinkle with seasonings. Pour
gravy over all. Cover and cook on low setting for 8 to 10 hours. During
the last hour of cooking, once chicken is very xender, stir in peas.
Serves 4.

Chicken on Sunday

Libby Hiatt
Michellville, IA

*This recipe is from one of our church cookbooks, submitted by
a very special lady in our church. Whenever I prepare it (not
necessarily on Sunday!), I remember her fondly.*

10-3/4 oz. can cream of
   mushroom soup
1-1/4 c. milk
3/4 c. long-cooking rice,
   uncooked

4-oz. can mushroom stems
   & pieces
1-1/2 oz. pkg. onion soup
   mix, divided
4 chicken breasts

Blend soup and milk in a bowl; reserve 1/2 cup of mixture. Add
remaining soup mixture to an ungreased 12"x8" baking pan; mix in
rice, mushrooms with liquid and half of soup mix. Arrange chicken
breasts on top. Spoon reserved soup mixture over chicken; sprinkle with
remaining soup mix. Cover and bake at 350 degrees for one hour.
Uncover; bake 15 minutes longer. Makes 4 servings.

Baked Ham with Brown Sugar Basting Sauce

Barb Rudyk
Alberta, Canada

This is the only basting sauce I use whenever I bake a ham. It always turns out juicy, never dried out! My mom used this ham basting recipe for years, so it's only natural that when I married, I continued using it.

5 to 6-lb. fully cooked bone-in
   ham
1/3 c. plus 1/2 c. water, divided
2/3 c. brown sugar, packed

1/3 c. vinegar
1 t. cinnamon
1/4 t. dry mustard

With a sharp knife, remove rind of ham; do not remove the layer of fat underneath. Cutting 1/4-inch deep, score fat all over in a one-inch diamond pattern. Place ham in an ungreased roasting pan; add 1/3 cup water to pan. Cover with aluminum foil; bake at 325 degrees for 30 minutes. Meanwhile, in a saucepan over medium heat, mix together remaining water and other ingredients. Bring to a boil; boil for 2 minutes. Remove ham from oven after 30 minutes; brush glaze over ham. Continue baking, uncovered, at 350 degrees for one hour, or until glaze is golden, basting occasionally. Remove ham to a serving platter; let stand for several minutes before slicing. Serves 10 to 12.

Baked sweet potatoes are delicious with baked ham. Pierce potatoes several times with a fork, and put them right on the oven rack. At 350 degrees, they'll be tender in about one hour. Top with butter and sprinkle with cinnamon-sugar. It couldn't be easier!

Fresh Strawberry Pie, page 184

Pecan-Raisin Cinnamon Rolls, page 26

Sleep-Over Breakfast Strata, page 8

Amanda's Garden Salsa, page 178

Italian Fried Green Tomatoes, page 79

Overnight Ham & Cheesies, page 157

Scalloped Potatoes & Ham, page 136

Tomato-Mozzarella Salad, page 71

Aunt B's Peach Freezer Jam, page 25

Deviled Eggs, page 158

Rainbow Pasta Salad, page 74

Pecan Pie Bars, page 205

Country Zucchini Bread, page 52

Favorite Spinach Dip, page 153

One-Pan Cabbage Roll Casserole, page 107

Mom's Chocolate Syrup Brownies, page 206

Dijon Chicken & Fresh Herbs, page 135

Grandpa John's Apple Cake, page 203

Mom's Baked Beans, page 90

Gram's Corn Flake Cookies, page 199

Ham & Bean Soup, page 42

Chicken & Wild Rice Soup, page 61

Irish Soda Bread, page 49

Supper Dishes

Slow-Cooker Smothered Steak

Marty Buxton
Clio, MI

This recipe has been a favorite birthday dinner request of my youngest daughter for many years. She's an adult now and has her own household, and still requests Mom to make this meal.

1-1/2 lbs. beef chuck or round
   steak, cut into strips
1/3 c. all-purpose flour
1 t. garlic salt
1/4 t. pepper
14-1/2 oz. can diced tomatoes
10-oz. pkg frozen French-style
   green beans

4-oz. can sliced mushrooms,
   drained
1 onion, sliced
1 to 2 green peppers, sliced
3 T. soy sauce
2 T. molasses
cooked rice or mashed potatoes

In a 4-quart slow cooker, combine steak strips, flour and seasonings. Stir well to coat steak. Add tomatoes with juice and remaining ingredients except rice or potatoes. Cover and cook on high setting for one hour. Turn to low setting; continue cooking for 7 hours, or until steak is very tender. Serve steak mixture ladled over cooked rice or mashed potatoes. Makes 6 servings.

Turn leftover mashed potatoes into tasty croquettes. Form into balls, dip into beaten egg and coat in dry bread crumbs, then fry in a little butter until golden on all sides.

Mamaw's Tuna Noodle Casserole *LaDeana Cooper*
Batavia, OH

There's nothing like turning to a comfort dish for a family dinner, looking around the table with a smile and remembering sitting across the table looking at your mom or grandma. It's those moments that warm my heart and make me love sharing some of my family recipes. We like our casserole saucy, so I double the soup, mayo and milk... yummy! I hope you enjoy this as much as my family and I do.

16-oz. pkg. wide egg noodles,
   uncooked
1 T. butter or olive oil
3 to 4 stalks celery with leaves,
   finely chopped
1/2 c. yellow onion, finely
   chopped
10-3/4 oz. can cream of
   mushroom soup
1/2 c. mayonnaise

1 c. milk
3 5-oz. cans tuna packed
   in water
1 t. garlic, minced
salt and pepper to taste
Optional: fire-roasted red
   peppers, frozen peas,
   steamed broccoli flowerets
Garnish: grated Parmesan cheese

Cook noodles according to package directions, just until tender; drain. Meanwhile, add butter or oil to a large saucepan over medium heat. Sauté celery and onion until softened but not mushy. In a large bowl, whisk together soup, mayonnaise and milk. Stir in celery mixture, undrained tuna, garlic, seasonings and optional ingredients, if desired. Fold in cooked noodles; transfer to a greased 13"x9" baking pan. Bake, uncovered, at 350 degrees for 20 minutes, or until bubbly and top starts turn golden. Sprinkle with Parmesan cheese. Makes 8 servings.

Pick up a bunch of sunny daisies at the grocery
store to tuck into a vintage milk bottle...
what could be sweeter on the supper table?

Grandma's Best
Supper Dishes

Creamy Clam Sauce & Vermicelli

Liz Blackstone
Racine, WI

My grandmother lived on Cape Cod, and we loved going to visit her every summer. Being from Wisconsin, it was just about the only time my siblings and I tasted clams! This is a favorite dish she made for us.

16-oz. pkg. vermicelli pasta,
   divided and uncooked
1/4 c. butter, sliced
1 c. sliced mushrooms
1/4 c. onion, finely chopped
1 clove garlic, chopped

2 T. all-purpose flour
2 6-1/2 oz. cans chopped clams,
   drained and liquid reserved
1 c. half-and-half
2 cubes chicken bouillon
1/4 c. grated Parmesan cheese

Cook half of pasta according to package directions; drain. Reserve uncooked pasta for use in another recipe. Meanwhile, melt butter in a large saucepan over medium heat. Add mushrooms, onion and garlic; cook until tender. Stir in flour. Gradually stir in reserved clam liquid, half-and-half; add bouillon cubes. Cook and stir until thickened. Add clams and Parmesan cheese; heat through but do not boil. Serve sauce over cooked pasta. Makes 4 servings.

Perfect pasta every time! Fill a large pot with water and bring to a rolling boil. Add one tablespoon of salt, if desired. Stir in pasta; return to a rolling boil. Boil, uncovered, for the time recommended on the package. There's no need to add oil...just stir often to keep the pasta from sticking together.

Slow-Cooker Pot Roast

Jennifer Bryant
Bowling Green, KY

Mom always made a pot roast on Sunday mornings when I was growing up. She would put it on early, and it would be ready when we came home from church. The house smelled wonderful! Then she would fix some corn or lima beans too, fresh from our garden. Sometimes I make pot roast in the oven like she did, but most often use our slow cooker. This roast will be fork-tender and the onion soup makes a nice gravy.

3-lb. beef chuck roast
4 baking potatoes, peeled and
   quartered
6 to 8 carrots, peeled and cut
   into 2 to 3 pieces

1 onion, quartered
salt and pepper to taste
1 to 2 T. olive oil
1/4 c. butter, sliced
1.35-oz. pkg. onion soup mix

Add roast to a 6-quart slow cooker sprayed with non-stick vegetable spray. Arrange vegetables around roast. Season with salt and pepper; drizzle olive oil over all and dot vegetables with butter. Sprinkle soup mix over all. Cover and cook on low setting for for 6 to 8 hours. After several hours, may spoon juices in slow cooker over vegetables once or twice. Makes 6 to 8 servings.

Grandma knew that cheaper cuts of beef like chuck roast and round steak are perfect for pot roast. They cook up fork-tender, juicy and flavorful...there's simply no need to purchase more expensive cuts.

Grandma's Best
Supper Dishes

Mom's 3-Cheese Lasagna

Tiffany Jones
Batesville, AR

I love my mom's lasagna. It has been my birthday dinner request every year for as long as I can remember! Now my daughter Elizabeth also loves "pasagna" as she calls it.

9 lasagna noodles, uncooked
1 lb. ground beef, browned
   and drained
2 24-oz. jars spaghetti sauce
16-oz. container large-curd
   cottage cheese
8-oz. pkg. shredded mozzarella
   cheese
1-1/2 c. grated Parmesan cheese
salt and pepper to taste

Cook lasagna noodles according to package directions; drain. In a large saucepan over medium-low heat, combine remaining ingredients; stir until cheese is melted. Remove from heat. Spread 1/4 of sauce mixture in the bottom of a greased deep 13"x9" baking pan; add 3 noodles. Continue layering twice, finish with sauce on top. Bake, uncovered, at 425 degrees for 15 to 20 minutes, until hot and bubbly. Makes 6 servings.

Aunt Nervy's Spaghetti Sauce

LuAnn Currier
Mount Vernon, OH

My mom's name was Minerva, but all my cousins called her "Aunt Nervy." This is her special spaghetti sauce that everyone loved!

29-oz. can tomato sauce
6-oz. can tomato paste
1/4 lb. pepperoni, diced
2 T. grated Parmesan cheese
2 T. sugar
2 T. dried parsley
1 t. dried oregano
1 t. dried basil
16-oz. pkg. spaghetti, cooked

Combine all ingredients except spaghetti in a large saucepan. Simmer for about 2 hours; stir often. Cook spaghetti according to package directions; drain. Serve spaghetti topped with sauce. Makes 4 to 6 servings.

Nina's Sweet-and-Sour Meatloaf

Melissa Dattoli
Richmond, VA

My mom makes the best meatloaf. It was my favorite growing up!

1 c. dry bread crumbs
8-oz. can tomato sauce
2 eggs, beaten
1 T. dried, minced onion
1 t. onion powder

1 t. garlic powder
1 t. salt
1/4 t. pepper
1-1/2 lbs. lean ground beef

In a large bowl, mix together all ingredients except beef; let stand for 2 minutes. Add beef; mix thoroughly and form into a loaf shape. Place in a lightly greased 9"x5" loaf pan. Bake, uncovered, at 350 degrees for one hour. Spoon Sweet-and-Sour Sauce over top of meatloaf. Return to oven for another 10 minutes, or until meatloaf is cooked through. Makes 6 servings.

Sweet-and-Sour Sauce:

8-oz. can tomato sauce
2 T. cider vinegar
2 t. mustard

2 T. light brown sugar, packed
1/2 c. sugar

Combine all ingredients in a small saucepan. Cook over medium heat, stirring often, until sauce comes to a boil.

Making a meatloaf? Place 2 slices of bread in the bottom of your loaf pan...it will absorb a lot of the grease. Just toss them away when you're done.

Grandma's Best
Supper Dishes

Aunt Betty's Hearty Casserole

Janis Parr
Ontario, Canada

*This is a delicious meal that feeds a large number of people
without a lot of effort. So satisfying!*

12-oz. pkg. penne pasta,
    uncooked
4 slices bacon
1 c. onion, chopped
1 c. celery, chopped
2 lbs. lean ground beef
salt and pepper to taste

2 14-oz. jars spaghetti sauce
2 10-3/4 oz. cans cream of
    mushroom soup
2 10-3/4 oz. cans cream of
    chicken soup
1 c. seasoned dry bread crumbs

Cook pasta according to package directions; drain. Meanwhile, in a large
skillet over medium heat, cook bacon until crisp; set aside bacon on
paper towels. Add onion and celery to drippings in skillet; cook until
tender and add to a greased 4-quart casserole dish. Brown beef in
skillet; drain and season with salt and pepper. Add beef and cooked
pasta to casserole. Pour spaghetti sauce over top; spoon soups over top.
Crumble bacon on top; stir mixture well. Cover and bake at 325 degrees
for one hour, or until hot and bubbly. Top with bread crumbs. Place
casserole, uncovered, under broiler for a few minutes, until crumbs are
golden. Makes 15 to 20 servings.

Do you have a new food jar that's really hard to open? Gently insert
the tip of a blunt table knife under the edge of the lid. That's usually
enough to break the vacuum, allowing the lid to twist right off.

Spicy Roast Chicken

Lori Rosenberg
University Heights, OH

It's a wonderful weekend meal, just like Grandma used to make.

2 t. olive oil
1 t. Italian seasoning
1 t. dried rosemary
1 t. dill weed
1 t. garlic, minced

1/2 t. ground cumin
1/2 t. salt
5-lb. roasting chicken, excess
    fat trimmed

Combine oil and seasonings in a small bowl; set aside. Starting at the neck cavity of chicken, loosen skin from breast and drumsticks by inserting your fingers, gently pushing between skin and meat. Rub seasoning mixture under loosened skin and over breast and drumsticks. Tie ends of legs together with kitchen twine. Tuck wing tips under chicken. Spray a roasting pan and rack with non-stick vegetable spray; place chicken, breast-side up, on rack. Bake, uncovered, at 450 degrees for 15 to 20 minutes. Reduce oven to 350 degrees. Continue cooking another 1-1/2 hours, or until a meat thermometer inserted in thickest part of thigh reads 165 degrees. Remove chicken to a serving platter; let stand 15 minutes before slicing. Serves 6.

A vintage large blue enamel roasting pan can handle plenty of kitchen tasks besides roasting. It's also terrific for oven-browning batches of meatballs, stirring up lots of snack mix...even set it over 2 stovetop burners and boil sweet corn for a crowd!

Grandma's Best
Supper Dishes

Dijon Chicken & Fresh Herbs

*Stacie Avner
Delaware, OH*

*I love making this family favorite in the summertime
with my fresh garden herbs.*

6 boneless, skinless chicken
   breasts
1/2 t. kosher salt
1 t. pepper

3 to 4 T. Dijon mustard
2 T. fresh rosemary, minced
2 T. fresh thyme, minced
2 T. fresh parsley, minced

Sprinkle chicken with salt and pepper. Grill over medium-high heat
6 minutes per side, or until juices run clear. Remove from grill and
brush both sides with mustard; sprinkle with herbs. Serves. 6

Picnic Fried Chicken

*Jason Keller
Carrollton, GA*

*Just like my grandma used to make in her big black cast-iron skillet!
She taught me not to crowd the skillet, even if you need to cook two
batches. Season with garlic powder and cayenne pepper, if you like.*

1/2 c. all-purpose flour
1 T. paprika
1-1/2 t. salt
1/2 t. pepper

3 to 3-1/2-lbs. chicken pieces
shortening or peanut oil for
   frying

In a shallow dish, mix flour and seasonings. Coat chicken with flour
mixture. Heat 1/4 inch of shortening or oil in a large skillet over
medium-high heat. Add chicken, skin-side down, and cook for 10 to
15 minutes, until lightly golden. Turn chicken over; reduce heat to low.
Simmer, uncovered, for 20 to 25 minutes without turning, until chicken
juices run clear when pierced. Serves 6 to 8.

Scalloped Potatoes & Ham

Michelle Powell
Valley, AL

Good old-fashioned comfort food! Using unpeeled potatoes, ham from the deli and pre-shredded cheese gets this dish into the oven in no time at all.

6 potatoes, sliced 3/8-inch thick
1 onion, thinly sliced and
   separated into rings
1-1/2 c. cooked ham, cut into
   small cubes
3/4 c. shredded mozzarella
   cheese
3/4 c. shredded Cheddar cheese
3/4 c. shredded Colby Jack cheese
6 T. all-purpose flour
1/4 c. butter, cut into small cubes
salt and pepper to taste
2 c. milk
5-oz. can evaporated milk

In a greased deep 13"x9" baking pan, layer potatoes, onion, ham and cheeses, making 2 or 3 layers. Sprinkle each layer with flour, dot with butter and season with salt and pepper. Combine milks; pour over layers. Season with more salt and pepper. Bake, uncovered, at 325 degrees for one hour, or until potatoes are fork-tender. Makes 6 servings.

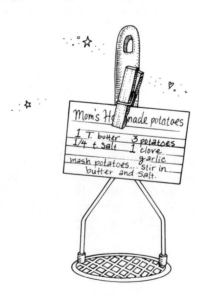

For a whimsical recipe card holder, hot-glue a clip clothespin to the handle of a tag-sale potato masher.

Grandma's Best
Supper Dishes

Slow-Cooker Pork Chop Noodles

April Tucker
Pensacola, FL

This dish was originally made in a skillet by my grandmother. The recipe has been handed down, and it is a comfort food we've eaten our whole lives. My sister adapted this recipe into a slow-cooker version, which fits our busy schedules better. Now, this is the only way we all make it. This dish freezes and reheats well.

2 T. butter
1/2 onion, diced
4 to 6 bone-in pork loin chops,
    preferably darker meat chops
salt and pepper to taste

2 28-oz. cans diced tomatoes,
    divided
16-oz. pkg. elbow macaroni,
    uncooked

Melt butter in a large skillet over medium heat. Sauté onion until just translucent. Season pork chops on both sides with salt and pepper; add to skillet. Cook until chops are lightly golden on both sides and onions are beginning to caramelize. To a 5-quart slow cooker, add 1/4 of one can of tomatoes with juice. Add 2 to 3 chops, 1/3 of onions and remaining tomatoes from can. Layer with remaining chops and onions; add remaining can of tomatoes with juice. Cover and cook on low setting for 7 to 8 hours, until chops are very tender. During the last hour of cooking, cook macaroni according to package directions; just until tender; drain. Discard bones from chops; add macaroni to slow cooker and stir well. Chops should be literally falling off the bone. Cover and cook for 30 to 45 minutes longer. Makes 4 to 6 servings.

To clean a cast-iron skillet after frying, simply scrub with coarse salt, wipe with a soft sponge, rinse and pat dry. No soap needed!

137

Polish Skillet Dinner

Pat Heney
Lexington, OH

This dish takes me back to eating in my Polish grandma's kitchen. It's an easy meal that can be whipped up in 20 minutes. Don't care for cabbage? Substitute green beans...it's just as good! May also substitute boiled potatoes for the noodles.

8-oz. pkg. medium egg noodles,
    uncooked
1 to 2 t. butter
1/2 white onion, coarsely diced
1 to 2 t. olive oil
1 clove garlic, minced

1 lb. smoked turkey sausage,
    cut into 3-inch pieces
1/4 c. water
1/2 head cabbage, coarsely
    chopped or shredded
salt and pepper to taste

Cook noodles according to package directions, just until tender; drain and stir in butter. Meanwhile, in a skillet over medium heat, sauté onion in oil. Add garlic and sauté just until tender. Add sausage and water to skillet; spread cabbage on top. Cover and cook over medium heat for about 14 minutes, until sausage is heated through and cabbage is tender, adding a little more water if necessary to prevent sticking. Add cooked noodles; toss with sausage and cabbage. Season with salt and pepper, as desired. Makes 4 servings.

Love cabbage, but not the aroma? Use an old-fashioned trick to keep your house sweet-smelling. Just add a spoonful of vinegar, a lemon wedge or half an apple to the cooking pot.

Grandma's Best
Supper Dishes

Gram's Best Stuffed Pork Chops

Sandy Coffey
Cincinnati, OH

This brings back fond memories of Grandma in her neat housedress and apron. It's one of the special Sunday dinners we enjoyed as kids, going to Grandma's house after Sunday School every week. We'd walk over and eat, stay awhile and then head home.

6 bone-in double-cut pork chops
2 c. soft bread crumbs
1 T. onion, grated
1 t. dried sage
3/4 t. salt
1/8 t. pepper
1 to 2 T. oil

With a sharp knife, cut a pocket between the bones in the side of each pork chop. Combine bread crumbs, onion and seasonings; mix well and stuff into chops. In a skillet over medium heat, brown chops in oil and a little water. Arrange chops in a lightly greased 14"x11" baking pan. Bake, uncovered, at 350 degrees for about one hour, until tender. Makes 6 servings.

Greek Lamb & Spaghetti

Darlene Neeley
Byrdstown, TN

This recipe is from my Greek grandfather. I remember my grandmother and my mother making it. For years I used cubed lamb, but now ground lamb is available, which simplifies it.

1 lb. lamb, ground or cubed
3/4 c. onion, chopped
2 to 3 t. olive oil
2 28-oz. cans diced tomatoes
10-3/4 oz. can tomato soup
1 T. Italian seasoning, or to taste
16-oz. pkg. spaghetti, uncooked
  and broken in half

In a stockpot over medium heat, cook lamb and onion in oil until no longer pink; drain. Add tomatoes with juice, soup, seasoning and enough water to fill pan halfway. Bring to a boil; add uncooked spaghetti. Add additional water as needed to keep spaghetti covered. Cook until spaghetti is tender, about 10 minutes. Serves 6 to 8.

Nana's Enchilada Pie

Chelsea Oliver
Arlington, TN

My nana used to make this recipe all the time for us...
whenever we asked her! It's delicious and reheats very well.

1-1/2 lbs. ground beef
1 onion, chopped
salt and pepper to taste
10-3/4 oz. can cream of
   mushroom soup
10-3/4 oz. can cream of
   chicken soup
10-oz. can mild enchilada sauce
4-oz. can chopped green chiles

3/4 c. milk
8 enchilada-size flour tortillas,
   divided
8-oz. pkg. shredded Cheddar
   cheese, divided
8-oz. pkg. shredded Monterey
   Jack cheese, divided
Optional: sour cream

In a large skillet over medium heat, brown beef with onion; drain.
Season with salt and pepper. Stir in soups, sauce, chiles and milk; set
aside. Line a greased 13"x9" baking pan with half of the tortillas. Top
with half of the beef mixture and half of the cheeses. Repeat layering.
Bake, uncovered, at 350 degrees for 40 minutes, or until hot and
bubbly. Let stand for several minutes; cut into squares. Top with sour
cream, if desired. Makes 8 to 10 servings.

After dinner, set up old-fashioned games like badminton and
croquet in the backyard...fun for all ages! Indoors, try favorite
board games. Everyone is sure to have a great time.

Gram's Mexican Chicken Casserole

Brandi Pixton
Martinez, CA

This casserole my grandma used to make for me for every birthday dinner I had. I always asked her to make this for me.

10-3/4 oz. can cream of
   chicken soup
10-3/4 oz. can cream of
   mushroom soup
1-1/4 c. milk
4-oz. can chopped green chiles
3/4 c. white onion, chopped
12 enchilada-size corn tortillas,
   cut into strips and divided

4 c. cooked chicken, chopped or
   shredded and divided
8-oz. pkg. shredded Monterey
   Jack cheese, divided
8-oz. pkg. shredded Cheddar
   cheese, divided

In a bowl, stir together soups, milk, chiles and onion. Spread a layer of soup mixture in the bottom of a lightly greased 13"x9" baking pan. Layer with 1/3 each of tortilla strips, chicken and remaining soup mixture; add 1/4 of cheeses. Repeat layering twice, ending with cheese. Cover with aluminum foil. Bake at 350 degrees for 40 minutes. Remove foil. Bake, uncovered, for remaining 20 minutes, or until cheese is bubbly and golden. Makes 8 to 10 servings.

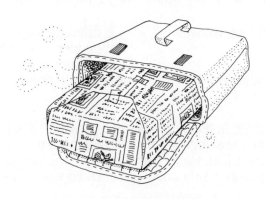

Taking a casserole to a potluck or carry-in dinner? Keep it hot by covering the casserole dish with aluminum foil, then wrapping it in several layers of newspaper.

141

Grandma Flossie's Italian Cod

Wendy Jo Minotte
Duluth, MN

This is a traditional Italian Christmas Eve dish, but we enjoy it year 'round. For the bread crumbs, I use the heels from loaves of bread, dried in the oven at 200 degrees and crushed with a rolling pin. I love to serve this with buttered rice and steamed fresh broccoli.

2-1/2 lbs. boneless, skinless cod
    loins, thawed if frozen
1 c. dry bread crumbs

1-1/2 t. granulated garlic
1/2 t. salt
1/4 c. olive oil

Arrange fish pieces side-by-side in a greased 13"x9" baking pan; set aside. In a small bowl, whisk together bread crumbs, garlic and salt. Add oil; mix thoroughly. Use your fingers to pat crumb mixture over fish. Bake, uncovered, at 350 degrees for 25 to 30 minutes, until fish is opaque in the center and flakes easily with a fork. Makes 8 servings.

Milk-Baked Fish

Lynn Williams
Muncie, IN

We ate fish every Friday when I was growing up, so Grandma knew a trick or two for making it tasty! The milk takes away any "fishy" flavor and makes the fish tender and sweet.

1-1/2 lbs. cod fillets, thawed
    if frozen
1-1/2 c. milk
1 leek, finely chopped
1 t. lemon pepper

1 t. dried parsley
hot pepper sauce to taste
salt to taste
1 lemon, halved

Pat fish dry; arrange in a single layer in a greased 13"x9" baking pan. Mix together remaining ingredients except lemon; pour over fish. Squeeze lemon over fish. Bake, uncovered, at 350 degrees for 15 to 20 minutes, until fish is firm and can be flaked with a fork. Makes 4 servings.

Grandma's Best
Supper Dishes

Shrimply Delicious Casserole

Kathy Van Daalen
New Smyrna Beach, FL

*I had a dear aunt who used to make this dish all the time.
She would sometimes substitute cooked chicken for the
shrimp. Either way, it was always delicious!*

12-oz. pkg. wide egg noodles,
  uncooked
2 10-3/4 oz. cans cream of
  chicken soup
2/3 c. mayonnaise
2/3 c. sour cream

1/2 c. green onions, sliced
1 T. dill weed
1 lb. cooked shrimp, peeled,
  cleaned and chopped
1-1/2 c. shredded sharp Cheddar
  cheese

Cook noodles according to package directions; drain. Meanwhile, in a
large bowl, combine soup, mayonnaise, sour cream, onions and dill
weed. Fold in shrimp and cooked noodles. Transfer mixture to a lightly
greased 13"x9" baking pan; top with cheese. Bake, uncovered, at
350 degrees for 30 minutes, or until bubbly and lightly golden.
Makes 4 to 6 servings.

Serve a tasty dill butter with crisp bread sticks. Soften 1/2 cup butter,
then blend in 2 teaspoons fresh dill weed, 2 teaspoons fresh chives
and one teaspoon lemon juice. Great with seafood!

Grandpa's Spaghetti Sauce

Amy Blanchard
Madison Heights, MI

My grandpa was a wonderful man who worked for years in an auto plant as a manager. He became good friends with a man who had immigrated from Italy. Grandpa got this recipe from his friend and it quickly became a family favorite. My grandpa passed away in 2006, and whenever I make this, I still think of him. This sauce is so good, I have eaten it without pasta, straight from the bowl. It's a very thick sauce...wonderful topped with Parmesan cheese!

6 onions, finely chopped
6 cloves garlic, finely chopped
1/2 to 3/4 c. fresh parsley,
   finely chopped
2 T. olive oil
5 lbs. ground beef round
1 lb. ground pork
6 6-oz. cans tomato paste

2-1/4 c. water
1 T. sugar
1/2 t. dried oregano
1/2 t. dried basil
2 T. salt
1 t. pepper
1 beef marrow bone

In a large stockpot over low heat, sauté onions, garlic and parsley in olive oil until soft. Add beef and pork; cook over medium-high heat until browned and any liquid is cooked out. In a bowl, stir together remaining ingredients except marrow bone; add to beef mixture. Stir well; bring to a boil. Reduce heat to low. Simmer for 3 to 4 hours, stirring occasionally. Add marrow bone; continue simmering for one additional hour. Makes 12 to 14 cups.

A whimsical centerpiece! Take a handful of long pasta like spaghetti, bucatini or curly strands of fusilli, and fan it out in a wide-mouthed vase.

Sloppy Joes

Catheryn Dottavio
Massillon, OH

My mother-in-law gave me this recipe years ago, and my children wouldn't eat any other kind of Sloppy Joes! Once they were grown up, they wanted this recipe for their own kids. This also makes a great coney sauce for hot dogs.

3 lbs. lean ground beef	3 T. brown sugar, packed
3/4 c. onion, chopped	3 T. Worcestershire sauce
3/4 c. green pepper, chopped	3 T. cider vinegar
2 10-3/4 oz. cans tomato soup	1 T. mustard
1/2 c. water	salt and pepper to taste
1 c. catsup	24 to 36 sandwich buns,split

In a large skillet over medium heat, brown beef with onion and green pepper; drain. Stir in remaining ingredients except buns; mix thoroughly. Transfer to a lightly greased 3-quart casserole dish. Bake, uncovered, at 375 degrees for one hour. To serve, spoon onto buns. Makes 2 to 3 dozen sandwiches.

Pick up a stack of vintage plastic burger baskets. Lined with crisp paper napkins, they're still such fun for serving burgers and fries... clean-up after dinner is a snap too!

Quick & Easy Hawaiian Hot Dogs

JoAnn Kurtz
Wichita Falls, TX

I got this recipe about 30 years ago. I was standing in line at the grocery store, and the lady in front of me shared it with me. I made it for my boys then, and now I make it for my grandkids. It's an easy favorite.

8 hot dogs
8-oz. can crushed pineapple,
   drained

8 slices bacon
8 hot dog buns, split

Slice hot dogs almost all the way through, creating a pocket. Stuff each hot dog with one tablespoon crushed pineapple. Wrap with one bacon slice, covering the whole hot dog. Grill or broil until bacon is crisp. Place each hot dog in a bun and serve. Makes 8 sandwiches.

Grandma's BBQ's

Heather Waite
Bryant, WI

This is a simple but tasty recipe that my grandmother handed down to me. I like to serve it on toasted hamburger buns with plenty of pickles.

1 lb. ground beef
1 onion, chopped
1/2 c. water
1/2 c. catsup

1-1/2 T. brown sugar, packed
1 T. Worcestershire sauce
1 T. vinegar
8 to 10 hamburger buns, split

Brown beef and onion in a skillet over medium heat; drain. Stir in remaining ingredients except buns; bring to a boil. Simmer over low heat for 15 to 20 minutes, stirring occasionally. To serve, spoon onto buns. Makes 8 to 10 sandwiches.

Set out stacks of colorful bandannas...they make super-size fun napkins when enjoying casual meals.

Grandma's Best
Supper Dishes

Granny's Hot Dogs & Potatoes

Dee LaRocco
Edgerton, WI

When I was growing up, there wasn't much money, same as a lot of people's childhoods. But mine differed in that my Granny and Papa took me in after my mother, their daughter, passed away. But I wasn't the only one they took in! Until I was a teenager, I honestly don't remember living in a house that was not filled with people. Someone (or a whole family!) was always coming to live with us for all kinds of reasons. I loved it! Granny had to get creative sometimes to make food stretch. This is just one of many family recipes that are good "stick-to-your-ribs" meals! It's also very easy to adjust, depending on the number of people you want to serve.

2 to 4 T. canola oil or butter
5 red potatoes, peeled if desired
    and cubed
1/2 red onion, diced

Optional: 1/4 each green,
    red and yellow pepper, diced
8 hot dogs, sliced 1/4-inch thick

Add 2 tablespoons oil to a cast-iron skillet; use butter for a non-stick skillet. Heat over medium-high heat. Add potatoes; cook until tender and lightly golden. Add remaining oil or butter as needed; cook onion and peppers, if using, until onion is translucent. Add hot dogs; cook until heated through and lightly browned, stirring often. Makes 4 to 6 servings.

Take dinner out to the back porch. Use old-fashioned pie tins as plates...serve up bottles of icy root beer and red pop from an ice-filled bucket. Just about anything tastes even better outdoors!

Runaway Dogs

Hope Davenport
Portland, TX

This recipe was originally called "Fried Devil Dogs," but when my mother-in-law shared the recipe with me, she explained how many years ago it got a funny name change. One day when my husband was just a little boy, he got very upset with his parents and decided he was going to run away. The only things he packed for his long journey were a change of clothes and the rest of the Devil Dogs his mom had cooked that day. Though it was not so funny at the time, everyone in the family now gets a good laugh when we talk about how Runaway Dogs got their name.

1 egg
1/2 c. milk
1 T. shortening, melted and
   cooled slightly
3/4 c. all-purpose flour
1/2 t. baking powder
1/2 t. salt

1/2 t. dry mustard
1/8 t. cayenne pepper
1/4 c. dry bread crumbs
6 to 8 hot dogs, cut into
   1-inch pieces
shortening for deep frying
Optional: horseradish sauce

In a bowl, beat egg slightly; stir in milk and melted shortening. In a separate bowl, whisk together flour, baking powder and seasonings. Add egg mixture; beat well. Spread bread crumbs on a plate. Dip hot dogs into bread crumbs and then into batter; set aside. In a skillet over medium-high heat, melt several inches shortening and heat to 375 degrees. Working in batches, add hot dogs; cook until golden on all sides. Drain on paper towels. Serve with horseradish sauce, if desired. Makes 6 servings.

No deep-frying thermometer? Here's how to tell when the oil is hot enough. Drop a bread cube into the hot oil...if it turns golden in 60 seconds, the oil is ready.

Fun Foods for
Get-Togethers

Hot Dried Beef Dip

Beth Flack
Terre Haute, IN

My grandmother used to make this irresistible dip every Christmas and New Year's. It was my grandfather's favorite.

8-oz. pkg. cream cheese, softened
8-oz. container sour cream
1/4 c. whole milk
1 T. cream-style prepared horseradish
1 t. Worcestershire sauce
1/2 c. red onion, finely chopped
1/2 c. celery, finely chopped
2 2-1/2 oz. pkgs. sliced dried beef, chopped
2 t. fresh dill, snipped
Garnish: chopped dill pickles crispy rye crackers or toasted party rye bread

In a large bowl, beat cream cheese with an electric mixer on low to medium speed until fluffy. Beat in sour cream, milk, horseradish and Worcestershire sauce until combined. Stir in onion, celery, dried beef and dill. Transfer mixture to a 1-1/2 quart slow cooker. Cover and cook on low setting for about 3 hours, until heated through. At serving time, stir; top with dill pickles. Serve with rye crackers or toasted party rye. Makes 24 servings.

Keep a bunch of fresh green parsley in the fridge, ready to add a little color anytime. Simply place the bunch, stems down, in a container of water and cover the top loosely with a sandwich bag. It'll stay fresh and flavorful up to a week.

Fun Foods for
Get-Togethers

Zippy Rye Teasers

Melissa Fialer
Palo Alto, CA

Whenever my stepmom found herself with guests coming for cocktails within the hour, she had a treasury of appetizer recipes on hand that could be made quickly and easily. This one has always been my favorite because it's so simple to assemble and bake. Substitute black olives for the green olives, if you like.

16-oz. pkg. party rye bread
8-oz. pkg. shredded Cheddar
   cheese
5 to 6 green onions, finely
   chopped

2-1/4 oz. jar sliced green olives
   with pimentos, drained
3 to 4 T. mayonnaise-type
   salad dressing

Arrange party rye bread on a baking sheet sprayed with non-stick vegetable spray; set aside. In a small bowl, combine remaining ingredients, adding enough salad dressing to make a moist consistency. Spoon mixture onto rye bread. Bake at 350 degrees for 10 to 12 minutes, until hot and bubbly. Makes 8 to 10 servings.

Make your own creamy yogurt cheese. Spoon plain unsweetened yogurt into a cheesecloth-lined colander and set it on a deep plate. Cover with plastic wrap and refrigerate overnight. The next day, season the fresh cheese with salt, pepper and chopped dill or chives. Mmm!

Grandma's Favorites

Herbed Cheese Spread

Vickie Wiseman
Hamilton, OH

This was one of my mom's favorite recipes for snacktime. It is so versatile and can be used in a lot of ways...terrific on bagels and hot baked potatoes. For a delicious chicken salad sandwich, use 3 cups of mayonnaise instead of the cream cheese and butter, then combine with 3 pounds of shredded chicken. Yum!

2 8-oz. pkgs. cream cheese, softened
1 c. butter, softened
2 to 3 cloves garlic, finely minced
1 t. dried oregano, or 1 T. fresh oregano, chopped
1/2 t. dried thyme, or 1-1/2 t. fresh thyme, chopped
1/2 t. dried basil, or 1-1/2 t. fresh basil, chopped
1/2 t. dill weed, or 1-1/2 t. fresh dill, chopped
1/2 t. white or black pepper

In a large bowl, blend cream cheese and butter together. Add herbs; gently mix well. Cover and refrigerate overnight before serving. Will keep for a week or more if covered and refrigerated. Serve at room temperature. Makes about 3 cups.

If you have a favorite busy-day recipe that calls for lots of different herbs or spices, measure them out into several small plastic zipping bags and label. Later, when time is short, just tip a bag into the mixing bowl.

Fun Foods for
Get-Togethers

Favorite Spinach Dip

Krista Marshall
Fort Wayne, IN

This is one of my favorite dips, and it comes from my grandma. She first made it at Thanksgiving a few years ago, and I couldn't stop eating it! The little bit of crunch added by the water chestnuts will have guests saying "Yum!"

10-oz. pkg. frozen chopped
    spinach, thawed and
    well-drained
16-oz. container sour cream
8-oz. can whole water chestnuts,
    drained and finely chopped

1/2 c. mayonnaise
1.8-oz. pkg. vegetable soup &
    dip mix
1 round loaf pumpernickel bread

In a large bowl, combine all ingredients except bread; mix well. Chill overnight. Slice off top of loaf; gently tear out center, reserving bread for dipping. Spoon dip into center of loaf. Serve chilled, surrounded with reserved bread pieces for dipping. Serves 8.

Jalapeño & Cream Cheese Spread

Heather Dondis
Richardson, TX

When I was young, we spent every Christmas at my grandmother's house in New Mexico. One year, my aunt made this very simple snack for us. It has been prepared many, many times since in our family, especially at Christmas. So simple, yet so delicious!

8-oz. pkg. cream cheese,
    softened
10-oz. jar red or green
    jalapeño jelly

round buttery crackers

Unwrap cream cheese and place on a serving platter. Spoon jelly over cheese. Surround with crackers and add a snack knife for spreading. Makes 8 servings.

Grandma Shirley's Party Meatballs

Naomi Townsend
Osage Beach, MO

My favorite grandma from our church group shared this slow-cooker recipe with me. A family favorite for many years, we serve this appetizer for potluck get-togethers and family dinners. It's handy to keep a package of meatballs in the freezer to use in this recipe, but you may also use your own homemade meatballs.

24-oz. pkg. frozen cocktail-size meatballs
1 c. catsup
1/2 c. sugar

1/2 c. water
6 T. onion, chopped
3 T. vinegar
2 T. Worcestershire sauce

Place meatballs in a 4-quart slow cooker; set aside. In a bowl, combine remaining ingredients and mix well; spoon over meatballs. Cover and cook on low setting for 3 hours, or until meatballs are cooked through, stirring occasionally. Serves 8 to 10.

Grandma always made you feel she had been waiting to see just you all day, and now the day was complete.
– Marcy DeMaree

Fun Foods for
Get-Togethers

Sausage Bread

Tina Goodpasture
Meadowview, VA

My Grandmother Hudson always had a table full of food, no matter what time of day you came into her kitchen. Meats, breads, apple butter, homemade apple turnovers...this lady loved to feed people! You had to eat something before you left. This bread is one of my favorites of hers.

16-oz. pkg. ground hot pork
   sausage
11-oz. tube refrigerated French
   bread dough

1-1/2 c. shredded pizza-blend
   cheese

Brown sausage in a large non-stick skillet over medium-high heat. Drain well, pressing between paper towels. Unroll dough into a rectangle on a lightly greased baking sheet; sprinkle evenly with sausage and cheese. Roll up jelly-roll fashion, beginning on one long side. Place on baking sheet, seam-side down; pinch ends to secure filling inside. With a sharp knife, cut 3 slits across the top, 1/4-inch deep. Bake at 350 degrees for 30 minutes, or until golden. Let stand for 10 minutes before slicing. Makes 6 servings.

Mama's Iced Tea

Mary Passafiume Hart
New Lenox, IL

My mom's iced tea and hospitality were enjoyed by many in our small town of Calumet. Our front porch was always filled with family & friends, enjoying conversation while sipping Mama's tea.

1 gal. cold water
12 to 16 t. unsweetened instant
   tea mix

1/2 to 3/4 c. lemon juice
3/4 to 1-1/2 c. sugar
ice cubes

Combine water and tea mix in a pitcher; stir well. Add lemon juice and sugar to taste; stir again. Refrigerate until chilled. Serve over ice. Makes 16 servings.

Great-Gram's Special Hamburger Sub Casserole

Sandy Coffey
Cincinnati, OH

Great for a get-together! This is super-easy, and you can make the spread ahead of time. Kids love it as well as adults. Serve with garlic bread and a tossed salad.

1 lb. ground beef
1/2 c. onion, chopped
1 c. water
salt and pepper to taste
32-oz. jar spaghetti sauce
12 slices bread

8-oz. pkg. cream cheese, softened
1/2 c. mayonnaise
1 T. Italian salad dressing
8-oz. pkg. favorite shredded cheese, divided

In a skillet over medium heat, cook beef with onion, water, salt and pepper until browned. Drain; stir in spaghetti sauce. Meanwhile, layer bread in a lightly greased 13"x9" baking pan. In a bowl, mix together cream cheese, mayonnaise and salad dressing; spread on the bread. Spread one cup shredded cheese over the bread; spoon beef mixture on top. Add remaining cheese. Bake, uncovered, at 350 degrees for 30 minutes, or until bubbly and cheese is melted. Makes 10 servings.

For a casual get-together, use empty tin cans with bright veggie labels to hold simple bouquets of black-eyed susans, zinnias and daisies. Line them up along the center of your table...charming!

Fun Foods for
Get-Togethers

Overnight Ham & Cheesies

Kimberly Newman
Peebles, OH

I first ate these tasty sandwiches at a church potluck...they didn't last long! They are quick & easy and delicious, perfect for any get-togethers since they are prepared the night before.

1 c. butter, sliced
2 T. honey mustard
1-1/2 T. Worcestershire sauce
1-1/2 T. poppy seed

1-1/2 T. dried, minced onion
2 12-packs Hawaiian rolls
1 lb. deli sliced baked ham
3/4 lb. sliced Swiss cheese

In a saucepan, mix butter, mustard, Worcestershire sauce, poppy seed and onion. Stir over low heat until blended and melted. Pour half of mixture into a lightly greased 13"x9" baking pan; set aside. Assemble sandwiches with rolls, ham and cheese. Arrange sandwiches in pan, spreading them around in sauce. Pour remaining sauce over buns. Cover and refrigerate overnight up to 24 hours. Bake at 350 degrees for 10 to 12 minutes, until golden and cheese is melted. Makes 2 dozen sandwiches.

Auntie Lillian's Party Punch

Daisy Sedalnick
Westminster, CO

This is the tastiest, easiest punch I have ever had. My brother-in-law's aunt gave me the recipe, and I have used it for numerous wedding and baby showers and after-parties. It's wonderful...I always make a double batch. Everyone loves it!

46-oz. can pineapple juice, chilled
6-oz. can frozen lemonade concentrate, thawed

3 2-ltr. bottles ginger ale, chilled
1 qt. raspberry, lime or pineapple sherbet

Combine all ingredients except sherbet in a large punch bowl; stir. Add scoops of sherbet just before serving. Makes 32 servings.

Deviled Eggs

Deanna Adams
Garland, TX

This is my grandmother's recipe, taught to me by my mother. The apple cider vinegar is the secret ingredient that gives them a special tang. A bit of hot pepper sauce is my own touch.

1 doz. eggs, hard-boiled, peeled
   and halved
1/2 c. mayonnaise
1 to 2 T. mustard
6 drops hot pepper sauce,
   or to taste
2 t. cider vinegar, or more
   to taste

1 t. salt
Optional: 1/4 t. garlic powder
Garnish: paprika, diced green
   onions, capers, pimento-
   stuffed green olives or
   bacon bits

Place egg yolks in a bowl. Arrange egg whites on a serving plate; set aside. Mash egg yolks with a fork. Add remaining ingredients except garnish; mix thoroughly. Adjust mustard, hot sauce and vinegar to taste and beat until smooth. With a spoon or a piping bag, fill each egg white with one to 1-1/2 teaspoons of yolk mixture. Garnish as desired; sprinkle with paprika and green onions, or top with 3 small capers, 1/2 pimento-stuffed olive or a sprinkle of bacon bits. Makes 2 dozen.

Planning to make deviled eggs? Use eggs that have been refrigerated at least 7 to 10 days. After boiling, pour off the hot water, replace with cold water and add some ice. The shells will slip off neatly.

Fun Foods for
Get-Togethers

3-Hour Refrigerator Pickles

Rhonda Darbro
Shell Knob, MO

These pickles are quick & easy to put together, with no canning process necessary. I received this recipe from a fellow Sunday School teacher. They are always a big hit whenever I fix them!

6 c. cucumbers, thinly sliced
3 small onions, thinly sliced
1 c. cider vinegar

1-3/4 c. sugar
2 T. salt
1/2 to 1 t. dill weed or dill seed

Combine cucumbers and onions in a large non-metallic bowl; set aside. In a separate bowl, combine remaining ingredients; stir well and pour over cucumber mixture. If necessary, add water to vinegar mixture, to completely cover cucumber mixture. Cover tightly and refrigerate for at least 3 hours before serving, stirring occasionally. May be kept refrigerated up to 3 months, or may be frozen after sugar has completely dissolved. Makes about 1-1/2 quarts.

If it's a beautiful day, take the party outdoors! Spread out a homespun quilt on the picnic table and enjoy the fresh air and sunshine.

Pickled Shrimp

Lynda Hart
Bluffdale, UT

My mother always made this recipe for family parties and holidays. I thought it was very gourmet and classy. It can be served with crackers or spooned over a salad.

1/2 to 1 lb. cooked medium shrimp, tails removed
1-1/2 c. cucumber, peeled and thinly sliced
3/4 c. onion, thinly sliced
1 c. olive oil

3/4 c. white vinegar
2 t. celery seed
1 t. salt
1/4 t. pepper
few drops hot pepper sauce

Combine shrimp, cucumber and onion in a bowl; set aside. In a separate bowl, whisk together remaining ingredients; pour over shrimp mixture. Cover and refrigerate for several hours before serving. Makes 4 to 6 servings.

Decorate a platter with radish roses. To make, trim off the stem end and root. Make 4 to 5 cuts around the radish, about 3/4 of the way through. Place in ice water for about 15 minutes, until the "petals" open.

Fun Foods for
Get-Togethers

Crabby Red Pepper Spread

Vickie
Gooseberry Patch

A favorite for get-togethers with my girlfriends...we love it!

8-oz. pkg. cream cheese, softened
2 6-oz. cans lump crabmeat, drained and flaked
1/2 c. shredded sharp Cheddar cheese
1/2 c. red pepper, finely chopped
1 T. Dijon mustard
2 green onions, thinly sliced and divided
buttery round crackers

Combine all ingredients except crackers, reserving 2 tablespoons onions. Mix well; cover and refrigerate for at least one hour. Garnish with remaining onions; serve with crackers. Serves 10.

Cheesy Crab Bites

Lori Brooks
Cumming, GA

These have been served at family gatherings since I was a little girl. My favorite aunt reminded me of this recipe once I had my own children and holiday meals to prepare...it brought me right back to my childhood! Serve on uncut English muffin halves for a nice luncheon item. The crab spread is good in omelets too.

8-oz. pkg. pasteurized process cheese
1/4 c. butter
6-oz. can lump crabmeat, drained and flaked
6 English muffins, halved and toasted

In a saucepan over low heat, melt cheese and butter together; stir in crabmeat. Cut each English muffin half into quarters. Top each toast triangle with cheese mixture; place on a baking sheet. Broil for one minute, or until bubbly and lightly golden. Serve immediately. Serves 8.

Betty's Deviled Ham & Cheese Ball

Dianne Ables
North Potomac, MD

My mother-in-law made this cheese ball for us whenever my family came to Oklahoma for a visit. We just couldn't get enough of this savory treat. Now my children want me to make it at our home!

2 8-oz. pkgs. cream cheese,
  softened
8-oz. pkg. shredded sharp
  Cheddar cheese
2-1/4 oz. can deviled ham
2 t. onion, grated
2 t. Worcestershire sauce
1 t. lemon juice

1 t. mustard
1/2 t. paprika
1/2 t. salt
2 T. fresh parsley, chopped
2 T. chopped pimentos, drained
1 c. chopped pecans
assorted crackers or thinly sliced
  toasted baguettes

In a large bowl, combine all ingredients except pecans, crackers and baguettes. Mix well; cover and chill until firm. Shape into a ball; roll in chopped pecans. Serve with crackers or toasted baguette slices. Makes 10 to 12 servings.

Primitive-style wooden cutting boards in fun shapes like pigs, fish or roosters can often be found at tag sales, or look for new ones at craft stores. They're fun to use as whimsical party snack servers.

Fun Foods for
Get-Togethers

Mom's Mustard Dip

Kim Smith
Greensburg, PA

This dip is great for pretzels, crackers and chicken strips. We love this so much that it has been used on chicken or ham sandwiches and none of my family even likes mustard! Be sure to use condensed milk, not evaporated.

14-oz. can sweetened condensed
  milk
1 c. spicy brown mustard

1 T. Worcestershire sauce
2 T. horseradish sauce, or
  to taste

In a bowl, mix all ingredients together. Cover and refrigerate. Makes 2-1/4 cups.

Yummy Biscuit Puffs

Amy Thomason Hunt
Traphill, NC

My husband loves snacking on these anytime. They taste like a soft pretzel!

1/4 c. butter, melted
2 T. grated Parmesan cheese
1 T. onion, minced

1-1/2 t. dried parsley
12-oz. tube refrigerated biscuits,
  quartered

In a shallow bowl, combine all ingredients except biscuits; mix well. Roll biscuit pieces in butter mixture. Place on a baking sheet sprayed with non-stick vegetable spray. Let stand for 25 minutes. Bake at 400 degrees for 8 to 10 minutes, until golden. Makes about 3 dozen.

Pick up a dozen pint-size Mason jars...perfect for serving frosty cold beverages at casual get-togethers with family & friends.

Grandma's Favorites

Grandma's Homemade Beef Stick
Andrea Nyers
Oregon, OH

This was always a family favorite, and the final recipe Grandma and I would make after all the holiday cookies were baked. I have continued this tradition for my own family...they love it too.

5 lbs. ground beef chuck
5 T. curing salt
1-1/2 T. mustard seed
1 t. garlic powder

1 t. red pepper flakes
1 T. pepper
1 t. smoke-flavored cooking
   sauce

Mix all ingredients in a very large bowl. Cover and refrigerate 8 hours or overnight. Mix again; form into 5 loaves. Put loaves on a large wire rack; set on a large rimmed baking sheet to catch drips. Bake, uncovered, at 170 degrees for 8 hours. Cool completely before slicing; wrap and keep refrigerated. Makes 5, one-pound loaves.

If you're planning a family get-together, decorate your table to bring back childhood memories. Glue photocopies of old family photos to heavy paper for personalized table centerpieces.

Fun Foods for
Get-Togethers

Grandma's Graduation Sandwiches

Helen Thoen
Manly, IA

This recipe came from my mother-in-law who made them for our family celebrations, especially high school graduation receptions. Our three sons love these and have dubbed the previously unnamed filling Graduation Sandwiches. A combination of beef and pork roasts can be used.

2 to 3-lb. beef chuck roast, trimmed
salt and pepper to taste
10-3/4 oz. can cream of chicken soup

salt and pepper to taste
14-oz. can beef broth, divided
2 doz. sandwich buns, split

Season roast on all sides with salt and pepper; place in a roasting pan. Bake, uncovered, at 350 degrees for 1-1/2 to 2 hours, or until very tender. Remove roast to a platter; cool completely. Grind roast in a food grinder; set aside in a bowl. In a saucepan over medium-low heat, cook and stir soup to a soft mixing consistency. In a large bowl, combine beef, soup, seasonings and just enough broth to make a spreading consistency. Cool; spread on buns. Makes 2 dozen.

An old-fashioned food grinder is handy for grinding meat for spreads, meatloaf and other recipes. To clean it easily when you've finished, just put a half-slice of bread through the grinder. The bread will remove any food particles.

Howdy-Do Bean Dip

Betty Lou Wright
Fort Worth, TX

Bean dip is a must for get-togethers, especially in Texas. My family likes this one because it's easy to make and stays warm in the slow cooker for grazing during college football season or the holidays. Use low-fat refried beans, cream cheese and sour cream to make the dip a bit healthier...it's still full of Texas-sized yumminess!

16-oz. can refried beans
1 c. salsa
1 c. shredded sharp Cheddar cheese
1 c. shredded Monterey Jack or Colby Jack cheese

1 c. sour cream
1/2 c. cream cheese, softened
1 to 2 t. taco seasoning mix
Garnish: chopped green onions
nacho tortilla chips or crackers

In a bowl, combine all ingredients except green onions and chips or crackers. Mix well with a spatula, or beat with an electric mixer on medium-low speed. Transfer mixture to a greased 3-quart slow cooker. Cover and cook on high setting for 1-1/2 hours. At serving time, stir; sprinkle with onions. Serve with tortilla chips or crackers. Makes about 5 cups.

Smoky Cheese Ball

Carol Maxfield
Hill City, SD

My Aunt Ethel makes this for us with lots of love. She gave me the recipe, and I added a little extra flavor.

2 8-oz. pkgs. cream cheese, room temperature
1-oz. pkg. ranch salad dressing mix
2 t. taco seasoning mix

1/4 t. smoke-flavored cooking sauce
2-1/2 c. finely shredded Colby Jack cheese, divided
assorted crackers

In a bowl, combine cream cheese, seasoning mixes and smoke flavoring. Stir in 2 cups shredded cheese. Form into a ball on a piece of plastic wrap; roll in remaining cheese. Wrap; refrigerate overnight. Serve with crackers. Makes 12 servings.

Fun Foods for
Get-Togethers

Grams' Taco Dip

Carilee Daniels
Newport, MI

My Grams made this for my graduation party, and now I make it all the time! It serves a crowd. I have tweaked it over the years, but I always have a high success rate when I bring this to a party!

2 16-oz. cans refried beans
1-1/4 oz. pkg. taco seasoning
   mix, divided
3 avocados, halved, pitted and
   sliced
2 T. lemon juice

2 16-oz. jars salsa
48-oz. container sour cream
2 8-oz. pkgs. shredded Cheddar
   cheese
8-oz. pkg. shredded Pepper Jack
   cheese

In an ungreased 13"x9" glass baking pan, mix refried beans and 2 tablespoons taco seasoning; spread in bottom of pan and set aside. In a bowl, mash together avocado and lemon juice; stir well and spoon over beans. Layer with salsa, sour cream and cheeses. Sprinkle remaining taco seasoning on top. Cover and refrigerate if not serving immediately. Makes 30 servings.

Vintage game boards make whimsical settings for game night buffets. Check the closet for forgotten games or pick some up at yard sales. Cover with self-adhesive clear plastic for wipe-clean ease.

Cream Cheese Sandwich Spread Bites

Joyce Roebuck
Jacksonville, TX

I have made these finger sandwiches numerous times for parties, showers and other get-togethers. They are really good...everyone is always surprised to find out that there is no kind of meat in them. I have shared this recipe with so many people.

2 8-oz. pkgs. cream cheese, softened
1/2 c. sour cream
1/4 c. mayonnaise-style salad dressing
1 c. pecans, finely chopped

1 green pepper, finely chopped
1/4 c. green onions, chopped
1 to 2 loaves bread, crusts removed
softened margarine to taste

In a bowl, blend cream cheese, sour cream and salad dressing until smooth. Stir in pecans, green pepper and onions; set aside. Spread each slice of bread thinly with margarine to keep the bread from getting soggy. Spread cream cheese mixture over bread; cut each slice into 4 strips. Makes 8 to 10 dozen.

To soften cream cheese quickly, unwrap and slice the bar
into 6 or 8 pieces. With more surface area,
it will take less time to soften.

Fun Foods for
Get-Togethers

Spinach Rolls

Kathleen Bell
Clovis, CA

I've been making these appetizer rolls for all our family & friends gatherings for years. Even though most of the guys are not spinach fans, they eat these up and expect them on the party table.

2 10-oz. pkgs frozen spinach,
   thawed and squeezed dry
8-oz. container sour cream
3/4 c. mayonnaise
1-oz. pkg. ranch salad dressing
   mix

1 c. real bacon bits
1/2 bunch green onions, finely
   chopped
12 large flour tortillas, cut
   into quarters

In a bowl, combine all ingredients except tortillas; mix until well blended. Spread evenly on each tortilla quarter. Starting at the long end of triangle, roll up tortillas to the pointed end. Cover and refrigerate until serving time. Makes 4 dozen.

Stuffed Cherry Tomatoes

Karen Gentry
Eubank, KY

These little tomatoes are really tasty...so pretty on a relish plate!

2 doz. cherry tomatoes
6 slices bacon, cooked and
   crumbled

1/2 c. green onions, chopped
1/4 c. cooked ham, chopped
1/2 c. mayonnaise

Cut a thin layer from top of each tomato. Scoop out pulp; set upside-down on a paper towel to drain. In a small bowl, combine remaining ingredients and mix well. Spoon mixture into tomatoes. Cover and chill. Makes 2 dozen.

Add extra texture to fresh veggies for snack trays...use a crinkle cutter to cut them into slices and sticks.

Aunt Jo's Nuts & Bolts

Ramona Wysong
Barlow, KY

My aunt gave me this recipe. It's always nice to have
something crunchy to snack on.

12-oz. pkg. bite-size crispy
   rice cereal
14-oz. pkg. bite-size crispy
   wheat cereal
12-oz. pkg. doughnut-shaped
   oat cereal

1 to 2 lbs. mixed nuts
12-oz. pkg. slim pretzel sticks,
   or more to taste
1 lb. butter
4 t. cayenne pepper
1-1/2 T. garlic powder, or to taste

Combine cereals, nuts and pretzels in a large container; toss to mix and
set aside. Melt butter in a saucepan over low heat; stir in remaining
ingredients. Drizzle butter mixture over cereal mixture. Toss to coat well;
spread in a shallow pan. Bake, uncovered, at 200 degrees for 3 hours,
tossing every 30 minutes to avoid overbrowning. Cool; store in an
airtight container. Makes 12 to 15 servings.

Serve up lots of snack mix, spooned into a punch bowl.
Add a scoop and a stack of snack-size paper bags...so easy
for everyone to help themselves!

Fun Foods for
Get-Togethers

Grammy's Best Caramel Corn

Sandra Smith
Lancaster, CA

I have been making this caramel corn for more than 25 years. Some friends have a standing-order request for it. I've tried a lot of different caramel corn recipes & this one is the best.

3 3.2-oz. pkgs. microwave
   popcorn, popped
Optional: 1 c. salted peanuts
2 c. brown sugar, packed

1 c. butter, sliced
1/2 c. light corn syrup
1 t. salt
1 t. baking soda

Measure 14 cups of popcorn into a large roasting pan; discard any unpopped kernels. Add peanuts, if using; toss to mix. Keep warm in a 200-degree oven. In a heavy saucepan over medium-high heat, mix together brown sugar, butter, corn syrup and salt. Bring to a boil, stirring occasionally. Boil without stirring for 5 minutes, until mixture reaches the hard-ball stage, or 250 to 269 degrees on a candy thermometer. Remove from heat. Add baking soda and stir well; mixture will foam. Pour over popped corn. Toss with buttered forks to distribute evenly. Bake, uncovered, at 200 degrees for one hour, stirring every 15 minutes. Cool completely; break into clusters. Store in a tightly covered container. Makes 3-1/2 quarts.

Stock up on festive party napkins, candles and table decorations at holiday sales. Tuck them away in a big box...you'll be all set to turn a casual get-together into a party.

Cool Vegetable Pizza

Leona Krivda
Belle Vernon, PA

This is a yummy recipe loved by young or old. Always a big hit wherever I take it!

2 8-oz. tubes refrigerated crescent rolls
2 8-oz. pkgs. cream cheese, softened
1 c. mayonnaise
1-oz. pkg. ranch salad dressing mix
3/4 c. red and/or green pepper, chopped

3/4 c. broccoli, chopped
3/4 c. cauliflower, chopped
1/2 c. green onion, thinly sliced
1/2 c. tomato, chopped
2-oz. can sliced black olives, drained well
1 carrot, peeled and shredded
1 c. shredded Cheddar cheese

Spread both tubes of crescent dough over an ungreased 11"x7" baking sheet. Bake at 375 degrees for 10 to 12 minutes, until golden; cool completely. In a large bowl, beat cream cheese, mayonnaise and dressing mix until light and fluffy. Spread over cooled crust. Top crust with all vegetables; sprinkle cheese over all. Cover with plastic wrap; refrigerate for several hours. To serve, cut into squares. Makes 20 servings.

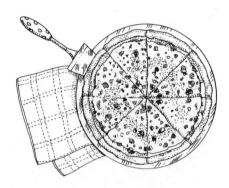

Let the kids help in the kitchen. Younger children can scrub vegetables and tear salad greens. Older kids can measure, chop, stir and take part in meal planning and shopping. Give 'em a chance...they may just surprise you!

Fun Foods for
Get-Togethers

Pimento Cheese Ball

Barbara Cave
Pilot Mountain, NC

This is a tried & true recipe I have used for over 35 years. I make it as an appetizer for guests or to take to others as a gift, especially at Christmastime.

12-oz. container pimento
  cheese spread
8-oz. pkg. cream cheese,
  softened
8-oz. pkg. sharp Cheddar cheese,
  freshly grated

1/2 t. garlic salt
1 t. pepper
Garnish: 1 c. chopped pecans
  and/or 2 T. paprika
snack crackers

Combine cheese spread, cream cheese and shredded cheese in a large bowl; let stand until room temperature. Add seasonings; mix well. Shape into one large ball or 2 smaller ones. Roll in pecans or paprika, or a combination of both. Wrap in plastic wrap; refrigerate overnight before serving. Serve with crackers. Makes 15 servings.

Prefer to shred cheese yourself? Place the wrapped block of cheese in the freezer for 15 minutes first...it will glide easily across the grater.

Helen's English Muffin Pizzas

Faye Lengenfelder
Renton, WA

This recipe from my friend Helen is more than 30 years old.
The muffin halves may be cut into quarters to serve as
appetizers, or left uncut to serve as a main dish.

1 c. shredded Cheddar cheese
1 c. mayonnaise
1 to 2 t. chili powder

2-1/4 oz. can chopped black
    olives, drained
6 English muffins, split

Combine all ingredients except muffins in a bowl; mix well. Spread mixture evenly on cut sides of muffins. Place muffins on an ungreased baking sheet. Bake at 425 degrees for 15 to 20 minutes, until bubbly and golden. Serve warm. Makes 6 to 12 servings.

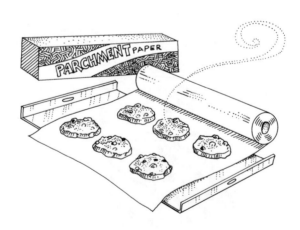

Sweet or savory treats won't stick to baking sheets
lined with parchment paper. Clean-up is a snap too...
just toss away the paper.

Fun Foods for
Get-Togethers

Grandmother's Sherbet Punch

Tammy Epperson
Nancy, KY

My grandmother always made this punch for all our special occasions. She lived to be 96 years old. We like it thick like a milkshake and drink it with a straw.

1- 1/2 gal. orange sherbet, softened
1-1/2 gal. pineapple sherbet, softened

1 ltr. ginger ale, chilled

Scoop sherbets into a punch bowl. Add enough ginger ale to make as thick or as thin as you like. Makes 10 servings.

Verna's Mud Sodas

Gladys Kielar
Whitehouse, OH

Mom made these mud sodas with us every summer, and we just loved them. It's an easy recipe kids can help make.

2 c. chocolate milk
2 c. root beer, chilled

1/2 pt. chocolate ice cream

To each of 4 tall glasses, add 1/2 cup of milk and 1/2 cup of root beer. Top each with 1/4 cup of ice cream. Serve immediately. Makes 4 servings.

Hosting a cookout for family & friends? Serve nostalgic soft drinks like root beer, orange pop and grape fizz in glass bottles, just for fun!

Grandma's Favorites

Chili Cheeseburgers

Brittany Jordan
Georgetown, TX

When I first got married, my husband told me about this recipe that his grandmother always made for him as a kid. Not knowing how to cook, I discovered that this simple recipe was always good and quick when even take-out got old. Also good with tortilla chips as a dip!

1 lb. ground beef
15-oz. can chili with beans
1 c. pasteurized process cheese
   spread, cubed

4 to 6 hamburger buns, split
   and lightly toasted

Brown beef in a skillet over medium heat; drain. Add chili and cheese. Cook, stirring often, until heated through and cheese is melted. To serve, spoon onto hamburger buns. Makes 4 to 6 servings.

Vintage tea towels make whimsical oversized napkins...handy for messy-but-tasty foods like barbecued ribs, buttered corn on the cob and juicy wedges of watermelon!

Fun Foods for
Get-Togethers

Smoky Burgers

Sheila Galus
Mantua, OH

*My grandfather made these burgers one day for us when we had
a summertime cookout. So easy and so good. Open up the foil
and you have a very juicy and tasty burger.*

1 lb. ground beef	1/2 t. pepper
1/2 t. garlic powder	1 onion, sliced
1/2 t. salt	4 hamburger buns, split

Mix beef and seasonings in a bowl; let stand for one hour to blend
flavors. Shape beef mixture into 4 patties; place each patty on a square
of aluminum foil. Place an onion slice on each patty; wrap up patties.
Place on a hot grill; cook for 30 to 45 minutes. Open foil carefully; place
burgers on buns. Makes 4 servings.

A diner-style meal is fun for the whole family! Make placemats
from vintage maps, roll up flatware in paper napkins and serve
catsup & mustard from plastic squeeze bottles.

Amanda's Garden Salsa

Violet Leonard
Chesapeake, VA

This is delicious! But be careful, it does have a kick to it. The recipe was passed down from my mother, who was the best cook ever, probably adapted by her from an old canning cookbook. You can also store this in the refrigerator if you don't want to can it. Just use it up within two months. If you like a thicker salsa, add a little less liquid.

2 lbs. tomatoes, peeled and
    chopped
12 fresh jalapeño peppers,
    seeds removed and chopped,
    or 7-oz. can jalapeño peppers,
    drained
1 onion, chopped
6 cloves garlic, minced

2 T. fresh cilantro, finely chopped
2 t. dried oregano
1-1/2 t. pickling salt
1/2 t. dried cumin
1 c. cider vinegar
3 1-pint canning jars and lids,
    sterilized

Combine all ingredients in a large stockpot. Bring to a boil over high heat; reduce heat to low. Simmer, uncovered, for 10 minutes. Ladle hot mixture into hot sterilized jars, leaving 1/4-inch headspace. Wipe rims; secure with lids and rings. Process in a boiling-water bath for 15 minutes. Set jars on a towel to cool. Check for seals. Makes 3 pints.

Mild, medium or spicy...salsa is scrumptious on so many foods. Jazz up plain burgers or hot dogs with a dollop of salsa instead of catsup. Turn eggs sunny-side up into huevos rancheros with a dollop of salsa and a sprinkling of cheese. Salsa can even be used as a fresh sauce for pasta!

Fun Foods for
Get-Togethers

Mom's Super-Quick Cheese Ball

Robyn Stroh
Calera, AL

*My mother always made this for our Christmas Eve and New Year's
Eve get-togethers. You can customize it with your favorite
flavor of salsa, and it's so easy!*

8-oz. pkg. cream cheese,
  softened
1/2 c. medium or hot salsa

8-oz. pkg. finely shredded sharp
  Cheddar cheese
1/2 c. chopped pecans

In a bowl, combine cream cheese and salsa until smooth. Add shredded
cheese. Line a separate bowl with plastic wrap; transfer cream cheese
mixture to bowl. Cover and refrigerate until firm. (May put into freezer
to speed up the process.) Lift cheese ball in plastic wrap onto the
counter; open up plastic wrap and sprinkle cheese ball with chopped
pecans. Roll cheese ball until covered with nuts. Re-wrap with plastic
wrap and return to refrigerator. Makes 10 to 12 servings.

Just for fun, spear cherry tomatoes or tiny gherkin pickles with
a toothpick and use to fasten party sandwiches.

Jezebel Spread

Elizabeth Smithson
Cunningham, KY

A friend brought this unusual spread to a Christmas party, and I just had to have the recipe! It's delicious on crackers...also good on baked ham and roast turkey.

8-oz. pkg. cream cheese,
  softened
2 t. prepared horseradish

2 t. mustard
1/2 to 2/3 c. apple jelly
1/2 to 2/3 c. pineapple preserves

Unwrap cream cheese and place on a serving plate; set aside. Mix remaining ingredients in a bowl. Spoon mixture over cream cheese. Makes 7 to 10 servings.

Creamy Fruit Dip

Kathy Courington
Canton, GA

My granddaughter loves to dip sliced fruit in this sweet spread. So easy and yummy!

8-oz. pkg. cream cheese,
  softened
3 T. frozen orange juice
  concentrate

7-oz. jar marshmallow creme
strawberries, sliced kiwi or other
  seasonal fruit

In a large bowl, beat cream cheese and orange juice until smooth. Fold in marshmallow creme. Serve with fruit. Keep refrigerated. Makes 8 to 10 servings.

Cute-as-a-button kitchen magnets! Look through Grandma's button box to find a variety of buttons. Hot-glue each button to a small magnet...ready to keep recipes and shopping lists handy on the fridge.

Fun Foods for
Get-Togethers

Rosemary-Feta Cheese Spread

Marilyn Gabler
Fort Worth, TX

I first took this appetizer spread to my garden club potluck for the holidays. Everyone loved it!

8-oz. pkg. cream cheese,
   softened
8-oz. block feta cheese, crumbled
chopped fresh rosemary to taste

2 T. jalapeño, apricot or
   fig preserves
snack crackers or melba toast

In a bowl, blend cheeses and desired amount of rosemary; form into a ball. Roll ball in additional rosemary; wrap in plastic wrap. At serving time, place cheese ball on a plate; top with preserves. Serve with crackers or melba toast. Makes 8 to 10 servings.

Nana's Strawberry Dip

Susan Smith
Pittston, PA

This simple recipe has been in our family my whole life. We just call it Strawberry Dip, but I figured in honor of my mom, we should give it the name "Nana's."

1/4 c. brown sugar, packed
3 T. orange flavor liqueur or
   orange juice
16-oz. container sour cream

hulled strawberries, pineapple
   cubes or other seasonal fruit
   for dipping

Combine brown sugar and liqueur or juice in a bowl. Stir in sour cream until smooth. Cover and refrigerate until ready to serve. To serve, set bowl on a platter; surround with fruit. Makes 8 servings.

Use a drinking straw to hull strawberries! Push the straw through the bottom end and the green, leafy top will pop right off.

Grandma's Favorites

Apricot-Peach Iced Tea

Eleanor Dionne
Beverly, MA

A favorite summer beverage when I was growing up. We had peach trees and my mom would make this for us every summer.

7 c. cold water
2 5-1/2 oz. cans apricot nectar
1 T. superfine sugar
3 family-size cold brew tea bags

1 lb. ripe peaches, sliced and
   pitted, or 16-oz. pkg. frozen
   sliced peaches, thawed
ice cubes

In a large pitcher, stir together water, apricot nectar and sugar. Add tea bags; let stand for 5 to 7 minutes, occasionally dunking tea bags, to desired strength. Discard tea bags. Add peaches; stir. Pour over ice and serve. Makes 8 servings.

Old-Fashioned Lemonade

Nola Coons
Gooseberry Patch

This recipe brings back summer memories of sipping lemonade on grandmother's porch.

6 lemons, divided
1 c. sugar
6 c. water, divided

ice cubes
Garnish: lemon slices,
   fresh mint sprigs

With a paring knife, cut the rind from one lemon into thin strips. In a small saucepan over medium-high heat, combine sugar and one cup water. Bring to a boil. Add lemon peel; simmer for 5 minutes. Remove from heat; let cool to room temperature and strain out peel. Halve and squeeze juice from all lemons. In a pitcher, combine lemon juice, remaining water and 1/2 cup sugar syrup. (Refrigerate remaining syrup for another pitcher.) Stir well. Serve over ice, garnished as desired. Makes 6 to 8 servings.

Big, colorful ice cubes for a party punch bowl!
Arrange thin slices of citrus in muffin tins,
fill with water and freeze.

Something Sweet
for You

Fresh Strawberry Pie

Eva Jo Hoyle
Mexico, MO

My family loves strawberries in the springtime. I love to make this fresh strawberry pie for them.

1-1/2 c. water
1 c. sugar
3 T. cornstarch
1/8 t. salt
3-oz. pkg. strawberry gelatin mix
1 T. lemon juice

1 t. red food coloring
4 c. fresh strawberries, hulled
　and sliced
9-inch pie crust, baked, or
　graham cracker crust
Optional: whipped cream

In a saucepan over medium heat, combine water, sugar, cornstarch and salt. Bring to a boil. Boil for 3 to 4 minutes, until mixture is clear. Stir in dry gelatin mix, lemon juice and food coloring. Remove from heat and set aside to cool. Arrange strawberries in baked crust. Pour cooled gelatin mixture over berries. Cover and refrigerate until set. Top with whipped cream, if desired. Serves 8.

Take Mom or Grandma along to a farmers' market and ask her
to share her tried & true fruit or veggie recipes with you.
You may find a new favorite or two!

Something Sweet
for You

Double-Good Blueberry Pie

Sara Tatham
Plymouth, NH

Our neighbor lady, Mrs. Fletcher, used to make scrumptious pies like this one years ago. I like this recipe better than the usual blueberry pie because most of the blueberries are uncooked. They taste fresh and flavorful in this wonderful pie!

9-inch pie crust, unbaked
3/4 c. sugar
3 T. cornstarch
1/8 t. salt
1/4 c. water

4 c. fresh blueberries, divided
1 T. butter
1 T. lemon juice
Garnish: whipped cream

Bake pie crust according to package directions; cool. Meanwhile, combine sugar, cornstarch and salt in a large saucepan over medium heat. Gradually stir in water and 2 cups blueberries. Cook, stirring constantly, until mixture comes to a boil. Continue to cook and stir for one minute, or until mixture is thickened and clear. Remove from heat; stir in butter and lemon juice. Allow mixture to cool; stir in remaining berries. Spoon mixture into baked pie crust, spreading evenly. Cover and chill for several hours before serving. Spread whipped cream over pie, or add a dollop to each slice. Makes 6 to 8 servings.

Shake up some whipped cream in a Mason jar! Add 1/2 to one cup whipping cream to a wide-mouth jar, close the lid tightly and shake vigorously for one to 2 minutes. Stir in a little sugar and vanilla, if you like.

Peach Upside-Down Cake

Tina Wright
Atlanta, GA

My Aunt Lillie was well-known for her wonderful pies and cakes.
When she brought this wonderful cake to a family picnic, we were in
seventh heaven! If you don't have a cast-iron skillet, just use a round
cake pan.

1/4 c. plus 1/3 c. butter, divided
1 c. light brown sugar, packed
29-oz. can sliced cling peaches,
    well drained
4 maraschino cherries, sliced
1/4 c. toasted sliced almonds
2/3 c. sugar

2 eggs, beaten
1-1/2 c. all-purpose flour
1 T. baking powder
1/4 t. salt
1-1/2 t. ground ginger
2/3 c. milk
Garnish: whipped cream

In a 9" cast-iron skillet over medium heat, melt 1/4 cup butter with
brown sugar. Cook and stir until sugar is dissolved. Remove from heat.
Arrange 3 peach slices in the center of skillet, forming a circle. Arrange
remaining slices in a sunburst effect. Scatter sliced cherries and almonds
around peach slices; set aside. In a large bowl, blend sugar and
remaining butter; beat in eggs. In a separate bowl, combine flour,
baking powder, salt and ginger; stir well. Add flour mixture to sugar
mixture alternately with milk; mix well. Gently pour batter into skillet
over peaches. Bake at 350 degrees for 35 to 40 minutes, until a
toothpick inserted in the center tests clean. Immediately invert a serving
plate over skillet; turn skillet upside-down over plate. Leave skillet over
cake for a few minutes; turn out cake. Serve warm with whipped cream.
Makes 8 servings.

For best results when baking, set out butter and eggs on the kitchen
counter an hour ahead of time, so they can come to room temperature.

Something Sweet for You

Mom's Cherry Cobbler

Sharon Bedwell
Georgetown, KY

This is just about the only dessert we had when I was growing up. Mom almost always used cherries, but other canned fruits may also be used.

1 c. self-rising flour
1 c. sugar
1 c. milk
14-oz. can tart cherries, drained
   and 1/4 c. juice reserved

1/2 c. butter
cinnamon-sugar to taste

Mix flour, sugar and milk in a bowl; pour into a greased 9"x9" baking pan. Pour cherries with reserved juice into the center of batter; do not stir. Slice butter over top; sprinkle with cinnamon-sugar. Bake at 350 degrees for 45 to 60 minutes, until bubbly and golden. Makes 6 servings.

Grandma Clark's Blackberry Cobbler

Jimmy Cox
Westfield, IN

It was always fun to be at Grandma Clark's house during berry season. She would take us out to help pick blackberries. Then once they were brought inside and cleaned, she would make her very simple and delicious blackberry cobbler. Yum!

1/3 c. butter
4 c. fresh blackberries
1 c. all-purpose flour

2 t. baking powder
1 c. sugar
3/4 c. milk

In a 13"x9" baking pan, melt butter in a 350-degree oven. In a bowl, mix together flour, baking powder, sugar and milk; pour batter over melted butter. Sprinkle blackberries on top. Bake at 350 degrees for about 40 minutes, until golden, watching closely to avoid burning. Makes 8 servings.

Make dessert a grand finale...serve it on your prettiest china!

Honey-Oatmeal Cake

Megan Brooks
Antioch, TN

Simple, yet simply scrumptious! An old family favorite...we used to wrap up slices of this cake to tuck in our picnic basket.

1 c. long-cooking oats, uncooked	1 t. baking soda
1/2 c. butter	3/4 t. salt
1-1/4 c. boiling water	1 t. cinnamon
1-1/2 c. honey	1/4 t. nutmeg
1 t. vanilla extract	Garnish: 16-oz. container
2 eggs, beaten	coconut-pecan frosting
1-3/4 c. whole-wheat flour	

Combine oats, butter and boiling water in a large bowl; stir well and let stand for 20 minutes. Add honey, vanilla and eggs; mix well. In a separate bowl, mix remaining ingredients except frosting. Add flour mixture to oat mixture; stir well. Pour into a greased and floured 13"x9" baking pan. Bake at 350 degrees for 30 to 40 degrees, until a toothpick tests done. Cool; spread with frosting. Makes 12 servings.

Grandma always said, "Never return a dish empty." Gather up dishes and plates that have been left behind, fill them with homebaked goodies and return them to their owners... they'll be pleasantly surprised!

Something Sweet for You

Pineapple-Glazed Cake

Linda Belon
Wintersville, OH

*An easy recipe that makes a big cake...perfect for
get-togethers and oh-so good.*

1 c. margarine
2 c. sugar
2 eggs, beaten
2 t. vanilla extract
2 t. baking soda

2 c. all-purpose flour
15-1/4 oz. can crushed
　pineapple, drained
1/2 c. sweetened flaked
　coconut

Blend margarine and sugar in a large bowl. Stir in eggs; blend in
remaining ingredients. Pour batter into a greased and floured
13"x9" baking pan. Bake at 350 degrees for 35 to 40 minutes, until
cake tests done with a toothpick. Remove from oven; pour Glaze
over warm cake. Makes 12 servings.

Glaze:

3/4 c. sugar
1/2 c. butter
1/4 c. evaporated milk

1/2 t. vanilla extract
1/2 c. chopped walnuts

Combine sugar, butter and evaporated milk in a saucepan. Bring to a
boil over medium heat; boil for 2 minutes. Add vanilla and nuts; stir
well. Use immediately.

When mixing up cake batter, set the bowl on a damp kitchen
towel. The bowl will stay nicely in place.

Banana Split Pie

Linda Rich
Bean Station, TN

This recipe has been in our family for 50 years! It's delicious and makes a beautiful presentation. The kids and grandkids love it! I use a large plastic food keeper to make it in.

2-1/2 c. graham cracker crumbs
1/2 c. sugar
1/2 c. butter, melted
16-oz. pkg. powdered sugar
2 eggs, beaten
1 c. margarine, softened
1 t. vanilla extract
1/2 c. lemon juice

5 to 6 ripe bananas, sliced
    1/4-inch thick
20-oz. can pineapple tidbits,
    drained
8-oz. container frozen whipped
    topping, thawed
Garnish: pecan halves, red and
    green maraschino cherries

In a bowl, combine graham crumbs, sugar and melted butter. Press into a 14" round food container to form a crust; set aside. In a separate bowl, combine powdered sugar, eggs, margarine and vanilla. Beat with an electric mixer on medium speed for 15 minutes. (This is a must.) Spread mixture over crust; set aside. Drizzle lemon juice over bananas and let stand several minutes. Drain; spread over sugar layer. Cover bananas with pineapple tidbits. Spread whipped topping over all. Garnish as desired with pecans and cherries. Cover and refrigerate 2 hours before serving. Makes 16 servings.

Invite family & friends to a Sunday afternoon dessert social!
Everyone brings a pie, a cake or another favorite dessert...
you provide the ice cream and whipped topping.

Something Sweet
for You

Grandma Krieger's Brownie Ice Cream Pie

Gladys Kielar
Whitehouse, OH

My grandmother's dessert is perfect for a summer day.

18-oz. pkg. chewy fudge
   brownie mix
2 eggs, beaten
1/2 c. oil
1/4 c. water

3/4 c. semi-sweet chocolate chips
9-inch pie crust, unbaked
10-oz. pkg. frozen sliced
   strawberries, thawed
Garnish: vanilla ice cream

Combine brownie mix, eggs, oil and water in a large bowl. Stir with a spoon until well blended, about 50 strokes. Stir in chocolate chips; spoon into unbaked crust. Bake at 350 degrees for 40 to 45 minutes, until set. Cool completely. Purée strawberries in a food processor or blender. Serve slices of pie topped with a scoop of ice cream and a drizzle of strawberry purée. Makes 6 servings.

Treat your sweetheart to a heart-shaped cake, no special pan needed. Divide cake batter for 2 layers into one 9" round cake pan and one 9" square baking pan. Bake. Cut the circle in half and place a half on either side of the square's corners. Frost and serve...so sweet!

Simple Chocolate Cake

Kathy Forest
Swanzey, NH

I have been using this recipe for over 40 years. It's quick and always delicious...moist with great chocolate flavor. So easy, you don't even have to grease the cake pan! And with no eggs or milk, it can even be considered vegan or vegetarian.

1-1/2 c. all-purpose flour	5 T. oil
1 c. sugar	1 T. vinegar
3 T. baking cocoa	1 t. vanilla extract
1 t. baking soda	1 c. cold water
1/8 t. salt	

Sift flour, sugar, cocoa, baking powder and salt into a large bowl. With a spoon, make 3 holes in flour mixture. Pour oil into first hole, vinegar in second hole and vanilla in third hole. Pour cold water over all; mix until evenly blended. Pour batter into an ungreased 9"x9" baking pan. Bake at 350 degrees for 35 to 40 minutes, until a toothpick inserted in the center tests done. May also divide batter among 12 muffin cups, filling 2/3 full; bake at 350 degrees for about 20 minutes. Makes 9 to 12 servings.

For blue-ribbon perfect chocolate cakes with no white streaks, use baking cocoa instead of flour to dust the greased pans.

Something Sweet for You

Whipping Cream Pound Cake

Heather Spears
Oriental, NC

This is my Nannie's recipe. She made it all the time when I was little. I would give anything for her to be here now to make one for me. It is so good with ice cream or just a glass of milk. Her secret was to start in a cold oven...and no peeking!

1 c. butter, softened
3 c. sugar
5 eggs

1 T. vanilla extract
3-1/2 c. cake flour, sifted
8-oz. container whipping cream

In a large bowl, blend butter and sugar well. Add eggs, one at a time, beating after each. Alternately add vanilla, flour and whipping cream; blend well. Pour batter into a greased and floured tube pan. Place pan in a cold oven; set temperature to 325 degrees. Bake for one hour and 20 minutes. Makes 10 to 12 servings.

Brown Sugar Shoo-Fly Cupcakes

Ed Smulski
Lyons, IL

This recipes takes me back to my childhood in Chicago circa the 1930s. It has been a family favorite for decades, a special treat in our house for Christmas.

4 c. all-purpose flour
2 c. brown sugar, packed
1/4 t. salt
1 c. cold butter

2 t. baking soda
2 c. boiling water
1 c. baking molasses

Combine flour, brown sugar and salt in a large bowl; mix well. With a large fork or pastry blender, cut in butter until crumbly. Set aside one cup for topping; add baking soda to remaining crumb mixture. Add water and molasses to batter; stir well. Spoon batter into paper-lined muffin cups, filling 2/3 full. Sprinkle with reserved crumb mixture. Bake at 350 degrees for 20 to 25 minutes, until a toothpick inserted in center tests clean. Cool for 10 to 15 minutes in pan; transfer to a wire rack. Cool completely. Makes 2 dozen.

Old-Fashioned Banana Pudding

Renee Johnson
Cookeville, TN

My grandmother always made this delicious banana pudding with meringue topping from scratch. It's just right, not too sweet. I like to make it just like she did. I always get rave reviews and often hear, "This is the best banana pudding I've ever had."

3 egg yolks	1/4 c. butter
1 c. sugar	1 t. vanilla extract
1/4 c. all-purpose flour	11-oz. pkg. vanilla wafers
1-1/2 c. milk	4 to 5 ripe bananas, sliced

Combine egg yolks, sugar, flour and milk in the top of a double boiler. Cook and stir over medium heat until thickened to a custard consistency. Remove from heat; blend in butter and vanilla. Place a layer of vanilla wafers and sliced bananas in an ungreased 9"x9" baking pan. Cover with a layer of custard; repeat layers, ending with custard. (Some vanilla wafers may be left over.) Make Meringue; spread over pudding, sealing to edges. Bake at 300 degrees for 15 to 20 minutes, until meringue is golden. Best served warm. Makes 8 to 10 servings.

Meringue:

3 egg whites	1/8 t. cream of tartar
6 T. sugar	

In a deep bowl, beat egg whites with an electric mixer on high speed until soft peaks form. Add sugar and cream of tartar; beat until stiff peaks form.

Keep a stash of aprons in big and little sizes for everyone who wants to help out in the kitchen!

Something Sweet
for You

Phylis's Whisper Pie

Carolyn Deckard
Bedford, IN

This was my favorite aunt's recipe that she made and took to Grandma's on Sundays. One of my family's favorite pies too... the recipe makes two pies, yet there is never any left over!

15-oz. can sweet cherries, drained and juice reserved
6-oz. can frozen lemonade concentrate
2 envs. unflavored gelatin
15-3/4 oz. can vanilla pudding

8-oz. container cream cheese, softened
8-oz. container frozen whipped topping, thawed and divided
2 9-inch graham cracker crusts

In a saucepan, combine reserved cherry juice, lemonade and gelatin. Let stand for one minute; cook and stir over medium heat until gelatin is dissolved, about 5 minutes. Set aside to cool completely. In a bowl, beat pudding and cream cheese until light and fluffy. Add gelatin mixture; mix well. Cover and refrigerate until mixture is partially set, mounding when dropped from a spoon. Add cherries and 3/4 of whipped topping; divide between crusts. Cover and chill until firm. At serving time, spread remaining topping over pies. Makes 2 pies; each serves 6.

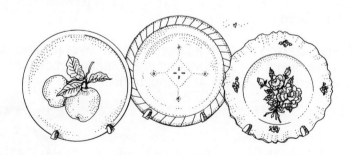

Garnish desserts with old-fashioned strawberry fans...so pretty! Starting at the tip, cut a strawberry into thin slices almost to the stem. Carefully spread slices to form a fan.

Aunt Teckla's Butter Cookies

Jennifer Waldeck
Orange, CA

These are easy and old-fashioned, rich, buttery cookies. They don't require any special cookie cutters or presses. I remember my grandmother's sister pressing these out with the patterned bottom of a glass tumbler!

2 eggs
2 t. vanilla extract
1/2 to 2/3 c. milk
2 c. butter, softened
1 c. sugar

1 c. brown sugar, packed
5 c. all-purpose flour
2 t. baking powder
1 t. baking soda

Beat eggs in a large glass measuring cup. Add vanilla and enough milk to make one cup; set aside. In a bowl, blend butter and sugars with a fork. Make a well in the center; add egg mixture. In a separate bowl, combine flour, baking powder and baking soda; mix well and add to butter mixture. Stir well. Form into balls the size of a small egg. Place on ungreased baking sheets; press down gently with a fork or the bottom of a glass. Bake at 400 degrees for 12 to 15 minutes. Cool completely on a wire rack; spread with Icing. Makes 3 dozen.

Icing:

1/2 c. milk
1 c. sugar
1/4 c. butter, sliced

1 t. vanilla extract
16-oz. pkg. powdered sugar

Heat milk and sugar to a boil in a large saucepan over medium-low heat, stirring until syrupy. Stir in butter and vanilla; remove from heat. Beat in powdered sugar, a little at a time, until smooth.

Keep cookies fresh longer...simply crumple some tissue paper and place it in the bottom of the cookie jar.

Something Sweet for You

Raspberry Thumbprints

Pamela Myers
Auburn, IN

My grandmother made these all the time, and they were my favorite cookies. They're so easy to make! Now, I make them during the holiday season, and they're always a big hit. I usually double the batch because they disappear so quickly.

1 c. butter, softened
1/2 c. powdered sugar
2 t. vanilla extract
2 c. all-purpose flour

1/4 t. salt
1/2 c. raspberry preserves
2 sqs. white melting chocolate

Add butter and powdered sugar to a large bowl. Beat with an electric mixer on medium speed until well blended. Beat in vanilla. Add flour and salt; blend well. Roll tablespoonfuls of dough into small balls. Place on lightly greased baking sheets, about one inch apart. Press down the center of each ball with a spoon, forming a thumbprint. Fill each with a teaspoon of preserves. Bake at 325 degrees for 15 to 20 minutes, until golden. Immediately transfer cookies to a wire rack to cool. Melt chocolate according to package directions; transfer to a small plastic zipping bag. Snip one corner of bag and drizzle chocolate over cookies. Let stand until set; store in a covered container. Makes 2 dozen.

If you see a vintage cake pan with a slide-on lid at a tag sale, snap it up! Not only is it indispensable for toting cake or cookie bars to a party, it also makes a clever lap tray for kids to carry along crayons and coloring books on car trips.

Great-Grandma's Ginger Cakes

Deborah Clouser
McLean, VA

My great-grandma was a Pennsylvania Dutch cook, and these soft cookies were always a family favorite!

2 c. mild baking molasses
3/4 c. shortening, room
   temperature
5 c. all-purpose flour
1 t. baking powder

1 t. baking soda
1 t. cream of tartar
1 t. ground ginger
3/4 c. sour milk or buttermilk

In a large bowl, mix together molasses and shortening; set aside. In a separate bowl, sift together all ingredients except milk. Add flour mixture to molasses mixture alternately with milk. Stir well to form a stiff dough; do not overmix. Add dough by teaspoonfuls to lightly greased baking sheets. Bake at 400 degrees for about 10 minutes, until no longer wet-looking. Cool cookies on baking sheets for one minute; transfer to wire racks. Makes 6 dozen.

Take time to invite a friend over for afternoon tea. Serve freshly baked cookies with a steaming pot of hot tea and spend time just catching up!

Something Sweet for You

Granny's Special Pecan Cookies

Donna Denkhaus
Fenton, MI

One of my grandma's best cookies. Love and miss her!

1 c. butter, softened
1/2 c. brown sugar, packed
1/2 t. vanilla extract
2 eggs, separated

1/2 t. salt
2-2/3 c. all-purpose flour
24 pecan halves

In a large bowl, blend butter, brown sugar, vanilla and egg yolks. Mix in salt and flour. Form dough into walnut-size balls; place on ungreased baking sheets. Beat egg whites and brush over cookies; press a pecan half onto each cookie. Bake at 375 degrees for 10 minutes. Makes 2 dozen.

Gram's Corn Flake Cookies

Elaine Conway
Buffalo, NY

My mom always made these delicious cookies to share with her great-grandkids. She has been gone for ten years now, but we still make them because they are a favorite of all.

5 to 6 c. corn flake cereal
11-oz. pkg. butterscotch chips

1/2 c. crunchy peanut butter

Place cereal in a large bowl; set aside. In a double boiler over low heat, melt butterscotch morsels and peanut butter; stir until smooth. Pour over cereal, stirring to well. Drop by teaspoonfuls onto wax paper; let stand until set. Makes 3 dozen.

Keep a collection of colored sugars and candy sprinkles on hand to make home-baked goodies special!

Grandma Buchsbaum's Special Birthday Cake

Sandy Rees
Quincy, IL

My grandmother made this cake every year for our birthdays. I'm so glad that my aunt had a copy of it so I can share it with my children. The day I received the recipe, I made it and it's just the way I remember it. The hardest part is to save it for birthdays only. It's so yummy!

1 c. butter, softened	4 t. baking powder
2 c. sugar	3/4 t. salt
4 eggs, lightly beaten	1 c. whole milk
3 c. cake flour	

In a large bowl, blend butter and sugar until smooth, about 5 minutes. Add eggs; mix until smooth and set aside. In a separate bowl, sift remaining ingredients except milk. Add flour mixture to butter mixture, alternating with milk. Divide batter between two, 8" round cake pans sprayed with non-stick vegetable spray with flour. Bake at 375 degrees for 30 minutes, or until a toothpick comes out clean. Turn out layers onto wire racks; cool. Assemble cake and frost with Chocolate Icing. Makes 16 servings.

Chocolate Icing:

6 sqs. unsweetened baking chocolate	1 t. vanilla extract
1/2 c. butter	16-oz. pkg. powdered sugar
	3 to 4 T. half-and-half

Melt chocolate and butter in a microwave or double boiler; add vanilla. Stir in powdered sugar. Add enough half-and-half to make a spreading consistency.

To neatly frost a layer cake, tuck strips of wax paper under the edges of the bottom layer. Discard the paper when the frosting is set.

Something Sweet for You

Homemade Ice Cream

Nan Calcagno
Grosse Tete, LA

As kids, we couldn't wait to take turns cranking our old-fashioned ice cream freezer, then taste the ice cream. Yummy! I still make this in summer for our grandkids and for us too.

6 eggs
1-1/2 c. sugar
2 T. cornstarch, or
    4 T. all-purpose flour
1/2 gal. whole milk

1/4 c. vanilla extract
3 12-oz. cans evaporated milk
14-oz. can sweetened
    condensed milk

Beat eggs in a large bowl. Add sugar and flour or cornstarch; stir until smooth. Add whole milk; whisk well and pour mixture into a large saucepan. Cook over medium heat, stirring constantly, until mixture comes to a bubbly boil. Remove from heat; add vanilla, evaporated milk and condensed milk. Stir well; allow to cool. Pour into an ice cream freezer. Freeze according to manufacturer's directions. Milk mixture may be made the day before and refrigerated until ready to freeze. Makes 12 to 15 servings.

Just-made homemade ice cream is scrumptious, but very soft.
For firmer, scoopable ice cream, immediately transfer it to
a plastic freezer container and place in the freezer compartment
for one hour to overnight...if you can wait that long!

Granny's Praline Cake

Elizabeth Smithson
Cunningham, KY

This recipe has been handed down from my great-grandma to my granny, my mom, myself and now my daughter. So easy and delicious!

2 c. all-purpose flour
1 c. sugar
1 t. baking soda
1/2 t. salt
2 eggs, beaten
20-oz. can crushed pineapple,
   drained

1-1/2 c. brown sugar, packed
   and divided
1 c. chopped pecans
8-oz. container whipping cream
1/2 c. butter
1 t. vanilla extract

In a large bowl, combine flour, sugar, baking soda, salt, eggs and pineapple. Mix well. Pour batter into a 13"x9" baking pan sprayed with non-stick vegetable spray. Top with one cup brown sugar and pecans. Bake at 350 degrees for 35 to 40 minutes. Meanwhile, combine remaining brown sugar, cream, butter and vanilla in a saucepan. Bring to a boil over medium heat, stirring often. Pour hot mixture over hot cake. Cool and refrigerate. Makes 8 to 10 servings.

A vintage hand-cranked mini food chopper makes short work of chopping nuts for cookies, muffins and other recipes.

Something Sweet
for You

Grandpa John's Apple Cake

Meghan Pankey
Yreka, CA

This was one of my grandfather's favorites! It became one of mine as well when I was little, and I'm the one who dubbed it "Grandpa John's." He passed away in 2007, but we always think of him while enjoying a nice slice of his apple cake. Delicious!

3 to 4 eggs
1 c. sugar
1 c. brown sugar, packed
3/4 c. oil
1 t. vanilla extract
2 c. all-purpose flour
1 t. baking soda

1 t. salt
1 t. cinnamon
4 c. Granny Smith or Fuji apples, peeled, cored and diced
Optional: 1 c. chopped pecans or walnuts
Garnish: powdered sugar

Beat eggs in a large bowl. Add sugars, oil and vanilla; stir well and set aside. In a separate bowl, blend together flour, baking soda, salt and cinnamon. Stir flour mixture into egg mixture; fold in apples. Add pecans or walnuts, if using. Pour batter into a greased 13"x9" baking pan. Bake at 350 degrees for 45 to 60 minutes. May also divide batter among muffin cups, filling 2/3 full; bake for 20 to 25 minutes. Sprinkle with powdered sugar, if desired. Serve warm or cold. Makes 16 to 20 servings.

Create a heavenly glaze for any apple dessert. Melt together
1/2 cup butterscotch chips, 2 tablespoons butter and
2 tablespoons whipping cream over low heat.

Halfway Squares

Nicole Draves
Pembroke, MA

This was my grandmother's most famous recipe. Everyone asked for the recipe whenever she brought these delicious bar cookies with their meringue topping to parties. Grandma has been gone many years, but people who knew her still talk about this amazing treat she made. I continue to make this dessert and think about her as I follow her handwritten recipe.

1 c. shortening, room
   temperature
1/2 c. sugar
1-1/2 c. light brown sugar,
   packed and divided
2 eggs, separated
1 T. water

1 t. vanilla extract
2 c. all-purpose flour
1/4 t. salt
1 t. baking powder
1/4 t. baking soda
6-oz. pkg. semi-sweet
   chocolate chips

In a large bowl, blend together shortening, sugar and 1/2 cup brown sugar. In a small bowl, beat egg yolks lightly with water and vanilla. Add to shortening mixture; set aside. In a separate bowl, sift together flour, salt, baking powder and baking soda. Add to shortening mixture; mix well. Press dough into the bottom of a ungreased rimmed baking sheet. Sprinkle chocolate chips on top. In another bowl, beat egg whites with an electric mixer on high speed until stiff peaks form. Add remaining brown sugar; beat well and spread over chocolate chips. Bake at 350 degrees for 20 to 25 minutes. Cool; cut into squares. Makes 15 servings.

The art of being happy lies in the power of extracting happiness from common things.
– Henry Ward Beecher

Something Sweet
for You

Pecan Pie Bars

Tammy Hill
Mishawaka, IN

As you may guess, pecan pie doesn't last long around eight kids! So my mom came up with these pecan bars that would last a little longer. Now that I'm a mom and a grandmother of eight, this is the way I make pecan pie stretch as well.

4 c. plus 2 T. all-purpose flour, divided
2 c. butter, softened
1 c. powdered sugar
1-1/2 t. salt, divided
6 eggs, beaten

1/2 c. butter, melted and cooled slightly
2 c. light corn syrup
1-1/2 c. brown sugar, packed
2 t. vanilla extract
1-1/2 c. chopped pecans

In a large bowl, combine 4 cups flour, softened butter, powdered sugar and 1/2 teaspoon salt. Mix well; press into a lightly greased 15"x10" jelly-roll pan. Bake at 350 degrees for 15 minutes; remove from oven. Meanwhile, in a separate bowl, combine remaining ingredients except pecans. Sprinkle baked crust with pecans; pour egg mixture over pecans. Bake at 350 degrees for 30 to 45 minutes, until topping is set. Cool at room temperature for one hour before cutting into squares. Makes 2-1/2 to 3 dozen.

Eggs work best in baking recipes when they're brought to room temperature first. If you're short on time, slip the eggs carefully into a bowl of lukewarm water and let stand for 15 minutes. They'll warm right up.

Mom's Chocolate Syrup Brownies

Vickie Wiseman
Liberty Township, OH

This was a favorite recipe around my house when I was growing up. The frosting is so good, you will be tempted to eat it straight from the bowl! Mom passed away in 1969, but her delicious recipe helps bring us memories of her.

1/2 c. butter	1 c. plus 1 T. all-purpose flour
1 c. sugar	16-oz. can chocolate syrup
4 eggs, beaten	Optional: 1/2 c. chopped nuts
1 t. vanilla extract	

In a large bowl, blend together butter and sugar well. Add eggs and stir well; add vanilla. Stir in flour; add chocolate syrup and mix well. Add nuts, if desired. Spread batter in a greased 15"x10" jelly-roll pan. Bake at 350 degrees for 30 minutes. Cool; spread with Frosting and cut into squares. Makes 2-1/2 dozen.

Frosting:

6 T. butter	1-1/2 c. sugar
6 T. milk	1/2 c. semi-sweet chocolate chips

Melt butter in a saucepan over medium-low heat; add milk and sugar. Stir well; bring to a boil. Boil for 2 to 3 minutes. Remove from heat; stir in chocolate chips until melted.

Save time when baking! Tuck a measuring cup into your countertop canisters. It'll be ready to scoop out flour and sugar in a jiffy.

Something Sweet for You

Little Gram's Cream Puffs

Beki Gonzalez
Moreno Valley, CA

My grandma always made these for me when I was a kid. To this day, whenever I smell them and eat them it takes me back!

1 c. water
1/2 c. butter
1 c. all-purpose flour
4 eggs, beaten

1 to 2 5-1/4 oz. pkgs. instant
   vanilla pudding mix
Garnish: powered sugar

In a 2-1/2-quart saucepan over medium heat, bring water and butter to a rolling boil. Stir in flour; reduce heat to low. Stir vigorously for about one minute, until mixture forms a ball; remove from heat. Beat in eggs; continue beating until smooth. On an ungreased baking sheet, drop dough by slightly less than 1/4 cupfuls, about 3 inches apart. Bake at 400 degrees for 35 to 40 minutes, until puffed and golden. Cool for 30 minutes. Meanwhile, prepare desired amount of pudding mix according to package directions; refrigerate at least 30 minutes, until set. Poke a hole in each puff; spoon in pudding. Dust with powdered sugar and serve. Makes about one dozen.

Elsie's Tea Cakes

Sharon Beaty
Boonville, IN

My Grandma Elsie was known for her beautiful roses, and she knew the names of all the varieties. She was also known for her charming, fancy tea parties with her lady friends. She was kind enough to share her secret tea cake recipe with her granddaughters.

1 c. butter, softened
1-1/2 c. sugar
4 eggs, beaten

1 T. almond extract
4-3/4 c. self-rising flour

In a large bowl, with an electric mixer on medium speed, beat butter and sugar; add eggs and extract. Slowly beat in flour to a dough consistency. Drop dough by tablespoonfuls onto baking sheets sprayed with non-stick vegetable spray. Bake at 350 degrees for about 10 minutes, until lightly golden. Makes 5 dozen.

Mama's Cheesecake

Diane Rullan
Quaker Hill, CT

My mom was given this recipe by her home economics teacher when she was in high school, 50 years ago. It has been made for the holidays almost every year since. Mom handed this recipe down to me and I have since shared it with my daughters. One of us usually makes it every year.

1-1/2 c. graham cracker crumbs
1/4 c. butter, melted
1 c. plus 1 T. sugar, divided
6 eggs, separated
2 8-oz. pkgs. cream cheese,
   room temperature

1 t. vanilla extract
1 t. lemon juice
16-oz. container sour cream,
   room temperature
Optional: 21-oz. can cherry
   pie filling

Preheat oven to 325 degrees. Fill a 13"x9" baking pan with water and place on the second shelf of the oven. For crust, mix together graham crackers, melted butter and one tablespoon sugar. Press into the bottom of a 9" round springform pan; refrigerate. In a separate bowl, with an electric mixer on high speed, beat egg whites until stiff peaks form; set aside. In another bowl, beat cream cheese and remaining sugar until light and fluffy. Add egg yolks, one at a time, mixing thoroughly. Add vanilla, lemon juice and sour cream; beat well. Fold in egg whites until well mixed. Pour filling into pan. Bake at 325 degrees for one hour. Turn off oven and open door slightly; leave in oven for one hour. Cover and refrigerate until chilled completely. At serving time, top cheesecake or individual slices with pie filling, if desired. Makes 8 servings.

Try something different for your favorite pie! Instead of graham crackers, use vanilla wafers, shortbread cookies or chocolate cookies to make a crumb crust.

Something Sweet
for You

Grandma Thompson's Delicious Lemon Pie

Barbara Cave
Pilot Mountain, NC

My grandmother passed away when I was in the fifth grade, and I am now a grandmother myself. My dad's youngest and last sister living is my Aunt Virginia. When her four daughters gave her a 75th birthday surprise party, she made this wonderful meringue-topped pie for us, and my family loved it. I was happy to be given the recipe, as I don't have anything else from my grandmother, and it is very special to me. Hope you like it as much as I do!

1 sleeve buttery round crackers	4 eggs, separated
2 14-oz. cans sweetened	1/4 c. sugar
condensed milk	1 t. cream of tartar
juice of 2 lemons	1 t. vanilla extract

Line a deep 2-quart round glass casserole dish with whole crackers; do not crush crackers. In a bowl, combine condensed milk, lemon juice and egg yolks; beat well. Pour into cracker crust and set aside. In a deep bowl, with an electric mixer on high speed, beat egg whites until fluffy. Add sugar, cream of tartar and vanilla; beat until well mixed. Spread mixture over pie, spreading to edges. Bake at 300 degrees for 15 minutes, or until meringue is set and lightly golden. Makes 8 servings.

A knife dipped in water makes cutting a meringue pie simple. There's no need to dry the knife between slices, just wet it again when the meringue begins to stick. So easy!

Canned Apple Pie Filling

Kelly Alderson
Erie, PA

My grandmother would take us kids to a pick-your-own orchard every fall, and we brought back bushels of apples. She turned them into all kinds of delicious baked goods...apple bread, apple brown betty, apple cookies, candy apples and, of course, apple pies. She'd save the rest by canning them. Her favorite apple was Granny Smith!

4-1/2 c. sugar
1 c. cornstarch
2 t. cinnamon
1/4 t. nutmeg
2 t. salt
10 c. water
3 T. lemon juice

Optional: 2 drops yellow food
   coloring
6 lbs. assorted apples, peeled,
   cored and sliced
7 1-quart canning jars and
   lids, sterilized

In a large stockpot, combine sugar, cornstarch, spices and salt. Add water; stir well. Bring to a boil over high heat; cook until bubbly, thickened and sugar is dissolved. Remove from heat; add lemon juice and food coloring, if desired. Pack apple slices into hot jars. Ladle hot mixture into jars, leaving 1/2-inch headspace. Gently remove any air bubbles with a knife. Wipe rims; secure with lids and rings. Process in a boiling-water bath for 20 minutes. Set jars on a towel to cool. Check for seals. Makes 7 quarts. Use 2 jars to make a 9-inch pie.

For delicious apple desserts, some of the best apple varieties are Granny Smith, Braeburn, Gala and Jonagold as well as old-timers like Rome Beauty and Northern Spy. Grandma's secret...for the best pies, use a mix of apple types.

Something Sweet
for You

Apple-Walnut Maple Conserve

Sherry Page
Akron, OH

A neighbor gave me this recipe years ago. It's great served hot, topped with vanilla ice cream for dessert. Use a food processor or blender to chop the apples, or simply use a knife.

6 lbs. Granny Smith apples, peeled, cored and coarsely chopped
4 c. sugar
2 c. brown sugar, packed
1 c. pure maple syrup

1 t. pumpkin pie spice
1 t. cinnamon
2 c. walnuts, toasted and finely chopped
11 1/2-pint canning jars and lids, sterilized

In a stockpot, combine all ingredients except walnuts. Bring to a boil over medium-high heat; reduce heat to low. Cook, uncovered, for 20 to 30 minutes, until thickened and apples are tender. Stir in walnuts. Return to a boil; cook and stir for 5 minutes. Ladle hot mixture into jars, leaving 1/4-inch headspace. Wipe rims; secure with lids and rings. Process in a boiling-water bath for 10 minutes. Set jars on a towel to cool. Check for seals. Makes 11, 1/2-pint jars.

Need a hostess gift in a jiffy? Fill a basket with hand-picked farmstand items...ripe fresh fruit, jars of jam or country-style cheese. Tie on a homespun bow, and she'll love it!

Grandma Emma's Cherry Drop Cookies

Leona Krivda
Belle Vernon, PA

Even though my Grandma Emma passed away before I was born, I feel I got to know her through her recipes that were handed down. This one has all kinds of goodies in it...walnuts, sweet cherries and coconut. Now her recipes will also be handed down to my daughters and my granddaughter.

3/4 c. shortening
1 c. brown sugar, packed
1 egg, beaten
1 t. vanilla extract
2 c. all-purpose flour
1/2 t. baking soda

1/2 t. salt
2 T. milk
1/2 c. chopped walnuts
1/2 c. maraschino cherries,
    well drained and chopped
1/4 c. sweetened flaked coconut

In a large bowl, blend shortening and brown sugar very well until light and creamy. Stir in egg and vanilla; set aside. In a separate bowl, sift flour, baking soda and salt together. Add flour mixture to shortening mixture alternately with milk; mix well. Fold in walnuts, cherries and coconut. Drop dough by teaspoonfuls onto lightly greased baking sheets. Bake at 350 degrees for 10 to 12 minutes, until golden. Makes 2 dozen.

A small scoop is so handy when making drop cookies. Just scoop the dough from the bowl and release it onto the baking sheet. So easy!

Something Sweet for You

Grandma's Chocolate Chip Cookies

Nancy Jay
Minster, OH

Grandma baked cookies one day every week. They were always hot out of the oven when school was out. We would stop by Grandma and Grandpa's house on the way home from school for a few cookies and a glass of milk. Making memories!

1 c. shortening
3/4 c. sugar
3/4 c. brown sugar, packed
2 eggs, beaten
2 T. milk
1-1/2 c. all-purpose flour
1 t. baking soda

1 t. salt
2 c. quick-cooking oats, uncooked
12-oz. pkg semi-sweet chocolate chips
Optional: 1 c. chopped pecans

In a bowl, stir shortening until softened; add sugars, eggs and milk. Mix until thoroughly blended and set aside. In a large bowl, sift together flour, baking soda and salt. Slowly fold flour mixture and oats into shortening mixture. Fold in chocolate chips and pecans, if using. Drop dough by teaspoonfuls onto ungreased baking sheets. Bake at 375 degrees for 10 to 12 minutes, until golden. Cool on wire racks. Makes 6 dozen.

Hosting a family reunion? Make bite-size desserts to share. Cupcakes, brownies and cookies are easy to snack on while everyone spends time catching up.

Fresh Gooseberry Pie

Naomi Townsend
Osage Beach, MO

Late in May of each year, my mother would take some old work gloves, cut off the finger tips for herself, my sister and me, and we would carry our buckets to the gooseberry patch. Those scratchy vines couldn't hurt our gloved fingers as we gathered the little green berries for some delicious pies!

3 c. fresh gooseberries, stemmed
1-1/2 c. sugar
3 T. quick-cooking tapioca,
    uncooked
1/4 t. salt

2 9-inch pie crusts, unbaked
2 T. butter, diced
Optional: small amounts milk,
    sugar

In a large saucepan, crush 1/2 cup gooseberries with a large spoon; add sugar, tapioca and salt. Stir in remaining whole berries. Cook and stir over medium heat until sugar is dissolved and mixture thickens. Line a 9" pie plate with one pie crust. Spoon in filling; dot with butter. Cover with remaining crust; seal and flute edges and cut several slits in crust. If desired, brush top crust lightly with milk; sprinkle with sugar. Cover edge with two long 3-inch wide strips of aluminum foil to prevent excessive browning. Bake at 425 degrees for 35 to 45 minutes, until crust is golden and juice begins to bubble through slits in crust. Remove foil during last 15 minutes of baking. Serve warm. Makes 6 servings.

An intricate lattice pie crust is glorious, but there's an easier way! Simply lay half the lattice strips across the pie filling in one direction, then lay the remaining strips at right angles. No weaving required!

Something Sweet
for You

Barbara's Buttermilk Pie

Amanda Ellerbe
Santa Anna, TX

My mother-in-law Barbara made this pie at every Thanksgiving and Christmas, and now I do too. It is delicious! I have even entered and won several pie bake-offs with this recipe. My family loves it. My children ask for it every year.

1/2 c. butter, room temperature
2 c. sugar
3 T. plus 1 t. all-purpose flour
3 eggs, beaten
1 c. buttermilk
1 t. vanilla extract
9-inch pie crust, unbaked

In a large bowl, blend together butter and sugar well. Add flour; cut in with a fork and blend well. Add eggs; beat well. Stir in buttermilk and vanilla. Pour mixture into unbaked pie crust. Bake at 350 degrees for 50 to 60 minutes, until a knife tip inserted into center of pie comes out clean. Makes 8 servings.

Lots of old-fashioned recipes call for buttermilk. If you don't usually have buttermilk in the fridge, though, a canister of powdered buttermilk is handy. Look for it alongside other shelf-stable milk products at the supermarket and keep it in the cupboard, ready to use anytime.

Nana's Blueberry Buttermilk Cake *Rebecca Reeves*
Endicott, NY

This recipe was passed down from my husband's paternal grandmother, fondly called Nana. My mother-in-law still makes this at least once a week, and the grandchildren gobble it up! It's yummy warm, with a glass of milk to wash it down. The recipe is very flexible...you can make it with blueberries, blackberries, raspberries or a combination of berries, even bananas or some jam swirled into the batter. Feel free to experiment!

3 c. all-purpose flour
2 c. sugar
1 c. shortening
1 t. salt
Optional: 1 to 2 t. cinnamon

1 T. baking powder
3 eggs, beaten
1 c. buttermilk
2 c. fresh blueberries

In a large bowl, mix together flour, sugar, shortening and salt with a fork until crumbly. Set aside one cup of crumb mixture for topping; if desired, mix cinnamon into reserved crumb mixture. Add baking powder to remaining crumb mixture. In a separate bowl, whisk together eggs and buttermilk. Add egg mixture to crumb mixture all at once; stir just until moistened. Batter will be lumpy. Gently fold in blueberries. Pour batter into a greased and floured 13"x9" baking pan, or divide between 2 greased and floured 8" round cake pans. Sprinkle evenly with reserved crumb topping. Bake at 350 degrees for 40 to 45 minutes for 13"x9" pan, or 30 to 35 minutes for 8" round pans, until a toothpick inserted in the center tests clean. Makes 24 to 32 servings.

Stock up during berry-picking season for delicious desserts year 'round. Lay unwashed berries on baking sheets and freeze, then pack into bags for the freezer. When you're ready to use them, rinse berries in a colander. They'll thaw quickly.

Something Sweet for You

Verna's Cherry Crunch Dessert *Barbara Hauenstein*
Forest City, PA

Our kids just loved it when our neighbor Verna would appear at the door with this delicious dessert! She would bring it over just to let us know she was thinking of us, and it became our favorite.

18-1/4 oz. pkg. white cake mix
1 t. lemon juice
1/2 c. butter, melted
Optional: 1/2 c. chopped nuts

21-oz. can cherry pie filling
Garnish: whipped cream or
    vanilla ice cream

In a large bowl, combine dry cake mix, lemon juice, melted butter and nuts, if using. Mix with a fork until crumbly. Spread half of crumb mixture in an 8"x8" baking pan sprayed with non-stick vegetable spray. Spread pie filling over crumb mixture; top with remaining crumb mixture. Bake at 350 degrees for 30 to 40 minutes, until golden on top. Cool in pan on a wire rack. Serve warm, garnished as desired. Makes 8 servings.

Serve ice cream-topped desserts to a party crowd,
the quick & easy way! Scoop the ice cream ahead of time
and freeze in muffin cups.

INDEX

INDEX

INDEX

Find Gooseberry Patch
wherever you are!

www.gooseberrypatch.com

Call us toll-free at 1·800·854·6673

U.S. to Metric Recipe Equivalents

Volume Measurements

1/4 teaspoon	1 mL
1/2 teaspoon	2 mL
1 teaspoon	5 mL
1 tablespoon = 3 teaspoons	15 mL
2 tablespoons = 1 fluid ounce	30 mL
1/4 cup	60 mL
1/3 cup	75 mL
1/2 cup = 4 fluid ounces	125 mL
1 cup = 8 fluid ounces	250 mL
2 cups = 1 pint =16 fluid ounces	500 mL
4 cups = 1 quart	1 L

Weights

1 ounce	30 g
4 ounces	120 g
8 ounces	225 g
16 ounces = 1 pound	450 g

Oven Temperatures

300° F	150° C
325° F	160° C
350° F	180° C
375° F	190° C
400° F	200° C
450° F	230° C

Baking Pan Sizes

Square		
8x8x2 inches	2 L = 20x20x5 cm	
9x9x2 inches	2.5 L = 23x23x5 cm	
Rectangular		
13x9x2 inches	3.5 L = 33x23x5 cm	

Loaf		
9x5x3 inches	2 L = 23x13x7 cm	
Round		
8x1-1/2 inches	1.2 L = 20x4 cm	
9x1-1/2 inches	1.5 L = 23x4 cm	